Sunshine & Storms

Discovery House Publishers is affiliated with RBC Ministries,
Grand Rapids, Michigan.

Requests for permission to quote from this book should be directed to:
Permissions Department, Discovery House Publishers,
P.O. Box 3566, Grand Rapids, MI 49501, or contact us by e-mail at
permissionsdept@dhp.org

Interior design by Sherri L. Hoffman
Interior photography: iStockphoto.com

ISBN: 978-1-57293-546-4

Printed in the United States of America

Second printing in 2013

Contents

Part 2: Standing Firm through the Storm

Abbreviations

CB   Crossing the Bridge Between You and Me
EBP   Everybody's Breaking Pieces Off of Me
LH   Life Is Like Licking Honey Off a Thorn
NR   No Rain, No Gain
WLT   When Life Takes What Matters
HW   When the Handwriting on the Wall Is in Brown
        Crayon

PART 1

Shining Like the Sun

*The righteous will shine like the sun
in the kingdom of their Father.*

Jesus, Matthew 13:43

What a Life

*My grandfather always said that living
is like licking honey off a thorn.*
Louis Adamic

*L*ife is sweet. It offers sunrises, fat baby fists, darting hummingbirds, outstretched arms, spring breezes, puppies, giggles, surprise parties, strawberries, voices in harmony, dimples, sheets on a clothesline, curls on little girls, compliments, fresh-baked bread, red wagons, great oak trees, whiskered men, love letters, pink parasols, marching bands, harvest time, feather pillows, waterfalls, boys on bikes, praise songs, full moons, cozy fires, communion, reunion, daisies, helping hands, pounding surf, butterflies, and white clouds mounded in blue skies.

Life is sharp. It pierces with good-byes, fevered brows, screams, empty beds, tornadoes and earthquakes, prejudice, poison ivy, traffic jams, tear-stained cheeks, ignorance, failure, war, drought, explosions, greed, lies, criticism, head-on collisions, rust and rot, floods, doubts, rejection, wrinkles, mosquitoes, hunger, hands that slap or steal, despair, divorce, rape, depression, broken bones, broken promises, broken dreams, broken hearts, broken lives, and dark clouds mounded in gray skies.

How can we enjoy the sweetness of this life without being pricked by its jagged thorns? How can we feel at home in a world blighted by sin yet blessed with the redeeming grace and presence of God?

God's children are not at home here; but we are *here*, nonetheless. And we discover that it's impossible to enjoy this world's sunshine without enduring its clouds and storms. There is no way to withdraw from only one part of life. Resistance to pain inevitably numbs us to joy.

So we accept the reality that this world of clashing darkness and light is where we are required to live and mature. Some day all things will be made new in Christ. But for now, our job is to stand firm and grow where we are planted by using all the sunshine and rain that comes our way. Would we come to harvest without either? *(NR)*

Jesus told [this] parable: "The kingdom of heaven is like a man who sowed good seed in his field. But while everyone was sleeping, his enemy came and sowed weeds among the wheat, and went away. When the wheat sprouted and formed heads, then the weeds also appeared.

12

"The owner's servants came to him and said, 'Sir, didn't you sow good seed in your field? Where then did the weeds come from?'

"'An enemy did this,' he replied. The servants asked him, 'Do you want us to go and pull them up?'

"'No,' he answered, 'because while you are pulling the weeds, you may root up the wheat with them. Let both grow together until the harvest. At that time I will tell the harvesters: First collect the weeds and tie them in bundles to be burned; then gather the wheat and bring it into my barn.'"

MATTHEW 13:24–30

A Family of Shining Realists

🌸

I want to make God smile, and I want to live before others so that when they see me, they will smile at God.

Dr. Amba Mputela

Some of us are born directly onto a bed of thorns. At least that's what it feels like. Our world hurts—seems always to have hurt. We are wounded and wary. Sometimes, justifying our rage at the neglect and abuse, we pass the hurt around. Life isn't fair in a fallen world.

Others, initially more fortunate, slide softly onto a bed of roses, and then discover with dismay that life's cozy cradle holds harsh thorns of reality. Things wilt and die. Sharp words and acts by unkind or unthinking people cut into self-worth and confidence. Loss slices through our world. We can become self-protective and guarded—filled with resentment that life turned and stung us. Life isn't fair in this sin-riddled world.

It is into such realities as these that our Savior was born. Jesus landed on a bed of scratchy stable straw, reaching out His hands for our spikes of sin, bowing His head to receive our crown of thorns. In Him the reality of righteousness met and conquered the reality of sin. But it was a painful battle. Jesus knew that sin was no small thorn. By our own choice, it had pierced us through the heart. And now, by His choice, it would pierce Him. Truly this wasn't fair. But God's amazing grace superseded "fairness." Mercy triumphed over justice.

Why did Jesus choose to make His bed on this earth? What prompted Him to accept such a painful assignment on our behalf? Why did He allow sin to stab Him to death, willingly taking our place?

In unfathomable love, Christ took our thorns of death to make of us a brand-new, eternal family of honest people, re-created in the image of God. He asks us to live transparently in the sweetness of His Spirit while still in this world of sin and brokenness. We are redeemed by our risen and living Savior, to shine like stars in the world's darkness. We are to offer the sweet fragrance of the hope of Christ to nostrils filled with the stench of death. We are to be like drops of honey, tempting a world to taste of God's eternal life and goodness.

Christ died to make us a family of shining realists . . .

- people who know where we're headed, but recognize we're not there yet.

- people who don't pretend that victory means lack of pain and struggle.
- people who laugh, and love, and give anyway.
- people who refuse to live in denial or fear.
- people willing to walk through the muck with Jesus.
- people who see clearly that the fruits of heaven and hell coexist on this earth.
- people who know that such a world offers great opportunity for God's grace.
- people who make God smile and live in a way that makes others smile at God.
- people who know how to lick honey off a thorn. *(LH)*

In this world you will have trouble. But take heart! I have overcome the world.

JESUS, JOHN 16:33

For this reason I kneel before the Father, from whom his whole family in heaven and on earth derives its name. I pray that out of his glorious riches he may strengthen you with power through his Spirit in your inner being, so that Christ may dwell in your hearts through faith . . . Be imitators of God, therefore, as dearly loved children, and live a life of love, just as Christ loved us and gave himself up for us as a fragrant offering and sacrifice to God.

EPHESIANS 3:14–17; 5:1–2

The Secret of Saying No

🌸

Simply let your "Yes" be "Yes," and your "No," "No."
Jesus, Matthew 5:37

If one of the tests for sanity is whether or not "voices" follow us wherever we go, most of us are in a whole lot of trouble. For it seems that on any given day, no matter which way we turn, some voice or another is demanding a chunk of who we are or what we can do.

A better test of sanity would be how we respond to the calls we hear. One of life's greatest challenges will always be in knowing which voice has a right to our time. When do I say yes?

Does every request have equal weight? Do we operate on a first come, first served basis? Are we easily persuaded and sidetracked because we have failed to define our priorities, commitments, and giftedness? Or do we have confidence and determination because we understand that by using God's gifts in God's way we will enhance our own lives as well as the lives of those we serve?

Once I was in a committee meeting where someone decided that the best way to fill positions was through bold assumption. "Don't you hear God calling you to be the youth leader?" that person asked, pointing at me from across the room.

"No, as a matter of fact, I don't even hear Him whispering!" I said with a smile.

It is easier to respond appropriately when we already are joyously using our gifts. But we also need to take into account our limitations . . . real, not imagined or self-imposed.

The truth is that my health, energy level, or lifestyle demands may be quite different from someone who is doing more than I am and suggesting that I do the same. So it falls to me to continually identify and honor my often shifting boundaries.

I may also find it difficult to say no when I want to please everyone, or be liked or needed, or thought of as wonderful and capable, and so my mouth may say, "Yes, of course I'll do it," while my mind is screaming, "Oh no, not one more thing!"

It is possible that someone, at some time, convinced me by word or example that a truly caring Christian should be able to do it all—and without a ripple of weariness or complaint. Therefore, if a person has a need and I have even an ounce of energy, a smidgeon of talent, or one moment of time, I feel as if I must accommodate the individual because saying no is uncharitable—not "nice."

Besides, if I say no I might feel responsible for their plight . . . who else will fill that position or do that job?

For all of these flawed reasons and more, a simple no can be very difficult for some of us to say and mean. The word sticks in our throats and chokes us.

But that only happens before we discover the marvelous secret that *inside every carefully thought-out "no" lies a resounding "yes!"*

"No, I can't go shopping right now, because I'm saying yes to an evening alone with my husband and children."

"No, I won't be able to head up that committee because I'm saying yes to some much needed quiet in my life right now."

We don't need to state our yes aloud. Our no, though small, can stand on its own when said firmly and pleasantly. The yes simply hides there to cancel any false guilt and offer positive direction and purpose to our choice. Yes is a powerful word, both when it is said wholeheartedly and when it is whispered from within a thoughtful no.

We can count on God to give us wisdom concerning all the voices calling for our time and energy. Then we can say yes with joy, and no with grace and confidence. *(EBP)*

Whether you turn to the right or to the left, your ears will hear a voice behind you, saying, "This is the way; walk in it."
ISAIAH 30:21

Love the Lord your God, listen to his voice, and hold fast to him. For the Lord is your life.

I will instruct you and teach you in the way you should go; I will counsel you and watch over you . . . Rejoice in the Lord and be glad, you righteous; sing, all you who are upright in heart!

PSALM 32:8, 11

I am always with you; you hold me by my right hand. You guide me with your counsel, and afterward you will take me into glory.

PSALM 73:23–24

To Name a Fear

*Who is more foolish, the child afraid of the
dark, or the man afraid of the light?*
Maurice Freehill

The subject of my Tuesday morning women's Bible study
class was fear, and it was with a certain amount of fear that
I went off to teach it because I knew I would have to begin
with a confession.

While preparing the lesson that week, I had reveled in
the satisfaction that I'm not a fearful person. I've never had
to wrestle with the vicious lions of fear that I've seen roar
through some people's lives and tear them apart.

Just about then the Lord poked His finger through the
veneer of my smug attitude, pointing out the sleeping cat that
I call Tabby. Instead of dealing with my fear, I made a pet out
of it. Instead of conquering it, I patted it on the head and fed
it saucers of milk!

How dangerous fear is when it purrs rather than roars. For when we don't recognize it as an enemy we allow it to curl up and stay on the hearth of our lives.

And while claiming that we're not "afraid," we are nevertheless concerned, worried, restless, anxious, bored, frequently sick, and unmotivated (or else working frantically). Or we feel guilty, indecisive, possessive, defensive, negative, shy, or tired—oh, so tired!

It takes a brave person to admit, "I'm worried because I'm afraid you'll . . ." "I can't choose because I fear that if . . ." "I'm so tired from working hard to prevent . . ." "I feel vulnerable when . . ." "But what if . . ."

The masks of fear are many and varied. They need to be uncovered and exposed to the Light of the World, who says, "Fear not!" For He knows how many things in this world evoke fear in His children.

When we're ready to call our fear by its first name, we're ready to receive Jesus' antidote to fear—which is simply (or sometimes not so simply) the faith to trust in Him. He is able. *(NR)*

Then he placed his right hand on me and said: "Do not be afraid. . . . I am the Living One; I was dead, and behold I am alive for ever and ever!"

REVELATION 1:17–18

The Lord is my light and my salvation—whom shall I fear? The Lord is the stronghold of my life—of whom shall I be afraid? When evil men advance against me to devour my flesh, when my enemies and my foes attack me, they will stumble and fall. Though an army besiege me, . . . even then will I be confident. . . . For in the day of trouble he will keep me safe in his dwelling; he will hide me in the shelter of his tabernacle and set me high upon a rock.

PSALM 27:1–3, 5

I sought the Lord, and he answered me; he delivered me from all my fears. Those who look to him are radiant; their faces are never covered with shame.

PSALM 34:4–5

The Place of Peace

*Sometimes being all wrapped up in God's
work becomes a substitute for being
all wrapped up in His presence.*

Octopus schedules
strangle us.
Escalating details,
    demanding deadlines,
    the strain of effort,
    suffocate and isolate.
Oh, to be held,
    rocked,
    freed
in the arms of a hug.
It takes a
    Special Friend
to give such an embrace . . .
One who said,
"Come unto Me

all you who labor and are
heavy laden,
    and I will give you rest."
One called
    Jesus.
Rest in him. *(EBP)*

———————— ❧ ————————

[Jesus] said to them, "Come with me by yourselves to a quiet place and get some rest."

MARK 6:31

For anyone who enters God's rest also rests from his own work, just as God did from his. Let us, therefore, make every effort to enter that rest.

HEBREWS 4:10–11

Grappling with the Pain of 9-11

Away from me, all you who do evil,
for the Lord has heard my weeping.

Psalm 6:8

Why do you think God permitted this Trade Center tragedy, Mom? Why didn't He prevent such a terrible thing?" my son asked.

"If only I knew," I said after a long pause. "This is so heartbreaking, and so difficult to understand. The depth and reach of the pain is almost unimaginable. But this has always been the big question, hasn't it? 'If God is so powerful, why does He allow sin and evil to run rampant? Why do good people suffer?'"

I told my son that while I certainly don't understand all the reasons evil is allowed its reign of terror in this world, I do know it doesn't mean that God is powerless. Then I was almost surprised to hear myself suggest that such tragedies reveal more about the nature of sin, and ultimately the nature of God's love, than they do about His power.

God's intention for us is always for good. He hates sin and death even more than we do. It breaks His loving heart that humanity invited sin into His perfect world, resulting in days like September 11, 2001. A horror like this, I began to understand, reveals to us that the cancer our rebellion against God brought into this world is so very awful, so pervasive and deadly, that to contain it God would have to do one of three things:

- Remove our free will.
- Wipe out the whole world and every sin-tainted thing and person in it.
- Do exactly what He is now doing.

Sin can only be "somewhat contained for a while" or "destroyed completely forever."

Those who continue to rebel against God and commit despicable acts perpetuate and escalate evil's terrible reign in our world. Tragedy is here because sinful people are here. Sinful people are here because God's love and grace are here, waiting and yearning for all to turn from deadly, dark evil and come to His light and love.

I can only conclude that if God doesn't rip away our free will, or wipe us out with no recourse—and it's important to realize that the integrity of His amazing love prevents Him from doing either of these things—then He can only do exactly what He is doing. Which is to first give of His own blood to solve our sin problem, and then to continue executing His long-range rescue plan that will one day chain up evil in a bottomless pit and establish a kingdom of righteousness forever. Meanwhile, He allows us time to come to salvation and eternal life in Jesus Christ.

The only possible reason we are still in the midst of this kind of pain is God's willingness to continue to suffer along with us, even after He paid sin's death-price for us. And He makes it clear that He does suffer with us, as His Spirit prays for us with groaning that cannot even be uttered. He waits to give us time to turn to Him and be saved eternally from the midst of it. We are being given time to come and bring others along.

It's important to remember that God already destroyed sin's power over us through His death and resurrection. Soon He will destroy the reality of sin's evil effect throughout creation. When that happens, there will be judgment for everyone who has sided with evil, eternally rejecting His gracious way of escape. *(LH)*

I am the way and the truth and the life. No one comes to the Father except through me.

JESUS, JOHN 14:6

Whoever comes to me I will never drive away. . . . For my Father's will is that everyone who looks to the Son and believes in him shall have eternal life, and I will raise him up at the last day.

JESUS, JOHN 6:37, 40

I tell you, now is the time of God's favor, now is the day of salvation.

2 CORINTHIANS 6:2

Cleansing the Wound

*The treatment the wound gets determines
whether time will bring healing or hate.*
Elsa McInnes, Shattered and Restored

When something of worth is taken from us, we are injured. If we lose something badly needed, highly valued, or deeply loved, the wound will be deep. If it was ripped away without warning, the laceration is jagged and raw. If it was slowly scraped away, the abrasion burns and stings.

Such wounds have one thing in common. They *hurt*. We don't like the pain, but it serves a purpose; it reminds us to treat and protect our injury. A thorough cleansing prevents serious infection, and a protective bandage shields the wound from further damage.

Emotional wounds demand the same careful attention as physical wounds, and the wounds of loss are especially vulnerable to contamination.

After the shock of losing her husband to cancer, Elsa McInnes discovered the painful truth that deep wounds can be breeding grounds for very unwelcome pests. She found that her normal and predictable emotions of sorrow, fear, and anger became infected with self-pity, blame, bitterness, and resentment. She writes in *Shattered and Restored*:

> Lord, . . . I marvel at the gentle distinction you made as you helped me face the contamination. You never once called grief a sin. You made a distinction between sin and the emotional wound that caused it. You showed me that you bind and heal emotional wounds with deep compassion. But then you gently pointed out that you can't treat destructive attitudes that find entry through those wounds the same way. There was no point in bathing them. They needed eviction notices and since the house they resided in was mine, it rested with me to tell them they were not welcome. Lord, right then I caught an uncomfortable glimpse of the wounds I was inflicting on your Holy Spirit as you tried to bandage mine.

Elsa's words hint that we may have work to do even while we are still dealing with pain, loss, and grief. We need to remain alert and close to God lest the Enemy find opportunity in our sorrow.

We may need to forgive something that seems unforgiveable. We may need to remind ourselves of how much God has forgiven us. Forgiveness begins with a choice and continues with daily, hourly, perhaps even moment-by-moment affirmations until it stands free—until *we* stand free.

We may be required to let go with grace when the time comes; to release what is being taken from us as well as the pain the loss leaves in its place. We may have to consciously choose healing and restoration and then verbalize what we want and need God to do for us. As we begin to express our desire to be whole and seek to obey His Word, we can rest in the truth that He knows what is best for us. He knows that we need cleansing, protection, healing, and restoration. He knows that we need *Him*. (WLT)

I am the Lord, who heals you.

EXODUS 15:26

When Jesus saw him lying there and learned that he had been in this condition for a long time, he asked him, "Do you want to get well?"

JOHN 5:6

Cleanse me with hyssop, and I will be clean; wash me, and I will be whiter than snow.

PSALM 51:7

Let all who take refuge in you be glad; let them ever sing for joy. Spread your protection over them, that those who love your name may rejoice in you.

PSALM 5:11

One of Those Days

As you know, we consider blessed
those who have persevered.

James 5:11

However uncharitable the thought, I find myself hoping that I am not the only one who has been required to live through days so bad that even Erma Bombeck wouldn't touch them with a ten-foot pencil. If I'm the only one, I've evidently been singled out for abuse in life, because—well, as humbly as I can say this—my level of expertise in this arena is hard to beat.

I know, for example, that it doesn't take a monumental crisis to make "one of those days"—just a series of common disasters and difficulties multiplied by the number of people living at your house. It's like being stoned to death with marbles.

In fact, usually it's the small stuff. The other day, one of our sons was chewing ice and his brother didn't want him to, so he said, "Stop that or I'll deck you," and he didn't so he did.

34

Add this sort of thing to spills, urgent phone calls, broken dates, skinned knees, frantic searches for keys, a hamster and a cat on the loose, overdue library books, and loud accusations that someone ate (or drank) the last of something that wasn't theirs and they had absolutely no right to do that and who do they think they are anyway . . . and we have the makings of the kind of day we hope to avoid but never can.

What really bothers me about this kind of day is not that Murphy's Law is having a heyday at my expense. It's that I happen to know that Jesus said, "By this all men will know that you are my disciples, if you love one another" (John 13:35).

On days like that, in fact all too often, I am tripping over anything and everything except love.

I'm not naïve enough to think that I should be able to get along splendidly at all times, with never a discouraging word, where "the skies are not cloudy all day." Even with only one foot in the real world I understand that in close relationships, things can get crowded. We're bound to bump into one another . . . and sometimes impatience and anger spill out. And sometimes the people closest to us form a combination that naturally generates sparks.

But if love can't always *keep* peace, it certainly knows how to *make* peace. Love knows the wisdom of a gentle word and a firm hand; the power of an apology and a hug; and the potential of a listening ear that hears and responds to the whimper of need beneath all the shouting.

Love also knows what *not* to do. On "one of those days," active love chooses not to take offense, not to get caught up in the emotional bedlam, not to keep score or flaunt a good memory, not to add to the problem.

But the trouble with such love is, and always has been, that God points His finger at *me* to start the cycle of love—even when I think it makes more sense for Him to make the other guy start, the one creating all the ruckus!

God said that love is patient, kind, gentle, full of hope, persevering, and fail-proof. But He never said love is easy—even when it comes from Him. (*EBP*)

———————— ❧ ————————

May the Lord direct your hearts into God's love and Christ's perseverance.

2 THESSALONIANS 3:5

Be imitators of God, therefore, as dearly loved children and live a life of love, just as Christ loved us and gave himself up for us as a fragrant offering and sacrifice to God . . . Live as children of light (for the fruit of the light consists in all goodness, righteousness and truth) and find out what pleases the Lord.

EPHESIANS 5:1–2, 8–10

May our Lord Jesus Christ himself and God our Father, who loved us and by his grace gave us eternal encour-

agement and good hope, encourage your hearts and strengthen you in every good deed and word.

2 THESSALONIANS 2:16–17

Caught in Life's Brambles

*Like fish taken in a cruel net, and like birds
caught in a snare, so mortals are snared at a time
of calamity, when it suddenly falls upon them.*

Ecclesiastes 9:12 NRSV

Imprisoned one,
    caught up in
    fears and failures,
    hopelessly ensnared,
try to remember . . .
Discouraged one,
    entangled in life's
    pain and problems,
    thinking no one cares,
try to remember . . .
When you can't find the way,

you need to find The Way.
Jesus is still
   The Way
      The Truth
         The Life.
He was your Way in
and He is your Way out.
Escape into His freedom.
Do this in remembrance of Him. *(LH)*

Jesus answered, "I am the way and the truth and the life. No one comes to the Father except through me."

JOHN 14:6

The Spirit of the Sovereign Lord is on me, because the Lord has anointed me to preach good news to the poor. He has sent me to bind up the brokenhearted, to proclaim freedom for the captives and release from darkness for the prisoners, to proclaim the year of the Lord's favor and the day of vengeance of our God, to comfort all who mourn, and provide for those who grieve in Zion—to bestow on them a crown of beauty instead of ashes, the oil of gladness instead of mourning, and a garment of praise instead of a spirit of despair.

ISAIAH 61:1–3

When Hope Is Crushed

Losing hope, painful as it may seem, is the way to discover hope.
David Augsburger, When Enough Is Enough

As we stood chatting after a meeting, a beautifully dressed woman of about fifty told me how deeply she was hurting. She hadn't known life could be so painful.

Until recently life had gone pretty much according to her plan. In fact, she had never been able to understand people who couldn't make life turn out right. She had met and married the perfect man, had sons who would make anyone proud, kept up a lovely home, attended church every Sunday, and found a nice job when the kids were grown. She had the formula: Live right and God will bless you with this kind of life. There was little she hoped for—except that life would continue to be this comfortable.

But it didn't. The bottom dropped out of her life and landed hard, crushing her hope for a perfect, pain-free existence.

When hope shatters, no matter how unrealistic it was, we become vulnerable to dangerous new hopes. For example, we may start to hope that, at the very least, we can rise above the pain. Isn't that what victorious living is all about? After all, God promised that we shall "mount up with wings like eagles" (Isaiah 40:31 TLB).

But life may clip the wings of even that hope, forcing us to walk the pathway covered by splinters of crushed hope. Soon our feet are sore and bleeding. At this point some folks, unable to see an end to the pathway of pain, settle for a scaled-down version of hope—a prescription that promises relief for inflamed feet. This hope expects relief—demands it in fact, reasoning that it's the very least God could do. This hope has been known to plan, scheme, bargain, demand, and even use Scripture out of context in an effort to twist the arm of God. This hope leads directly to disillusionment.

True hope focuses not on plans and prescriptions but on the person of God.

This living hope takes root in the reality of pain and holds us close to our Father who "did not spare his own Son, but gave him up for us all" (Romans 8:32).

This honest hope keeps its eyes wide open and its feet firmly planted in God's unfailing promises. All of them.

This patient hope does not demand to soar; it gratefully settles for "walking without fainting."

This sustaining hope opens the door to God's healing for my hurt, God's purpose through my pain, God's rest in my struggle, God's Word for my questions, and God's peace in the midst of my storm.

This eternal hope leads directly to heaven.

False hope expects to find relief *from* suffering. True hope expects to find God *in* suffering. (WLT)

Hope does not disappoint us, because God has poured out his love into our hearts by the Holy Spirit, whom he has given us.

ROMANS 5:5

Let us draw near to God with a sincere heart in full assurance of faith, having our hearts sprinkled to cleanse us from a guilty conscience and having our bodies washed with pure water. Let us hold unswervingly to the hope we profess, for he who promised is faithful.

HEBREWS 10:22–23

So do not throw away your confidence; it will be richly rewarded. You need to persevere so that when you have done the will of God, you will receive what he has promised.

HEBREWS 10:35–36

May the God of hope fill you with all joy and peace as you trust in him, so that you may overflow with hope by the power of the Holy Spirit.

ROMANS 15:13

The Pressure's On

Stress is our personal reaction to pressure.

Some time ago I conducted an informal survey. I polled a number of people regarding the stress in their lives. Here—in no particular order—are some of the things they claim cause stress:

Finances; sibling rivalry; computers; jobs (or the lack of one); punctuality; pain and illness; weeds and dirt; clutter; criticism and rejection; hormones; interruptions; relational difficulties; telephones (and being "on hold"); final exams; failure; lousy drivers; red lights (especially when they're flashing in the rearview mirror!); having to get up in the morning; wrinkles and gray hairs; noise; 97 percent humidity; machines, cars (and bodies) that break down; chairing a committee; opinions and expectations; separation; commercials; junk mail; repetitious duties; the neighbor's wind chimes; reading the newspaper; clocks; calendars; change; crisis; and a dog, a cat, two birds, and a family of gerbils!

A few people said things like poor attitudes, a sense of inadequacy, indecision, procrastination, and inflexibility. I give those people credit for both honesty and insight, because I believe they are close to the heart of the matter.

One man responded to my query with a question of his own. "What's the difference between pressure and stress?" he asked.

After a fascinating discussion we decided that all the external annoyances and difficulties that people named—such as noise, illness, interruptions, schedules, and crisis—are pressures. Stress enters the picture when these inevitable problems collide with unhealthy internal reactions—such as bad attitudes and habits, narrow perspective, unrealistic expectations, misconceptions, the need to control, denial, and resistance to change and growth.

When we understand that stress results from our personal reaction to pressure, we realize how desperately we need to be changed from the inside out. And this adds more stress because we know we are incapable of changing our own hearts.

Gently, God reminds us that the job is His. We are called to trust Him, cooperate with Him, and praise Him for His mighty works. He is able. But are we able to rest . . . and enjoy Him in the process? (EBP)

Praise be to the Lord, for he has heard my cry for mercy. The Lord is my strength and my shield; my heart trusts in him, and I am helped. My heart leaps for joy and I will give thanks to him in song. The Lord is the strength of his people, a fortress of salvation for his anointed one. Save your people and bless your inheritance; be their shepherd and carry them forever.

PSALM 28:6–9

The Lord is my shepherd, I shall not be in want. He makes me lie down in green pastures, he leads me beside quiet waters, he restores my soul. He guides me in paths of righteousness for his name's sake . . . Surely goodness and love will follow me all the days of my life, and I will dwell in the house of the Lord forever.

PSALM 23:1–3, 6

Remove This Thorn!

*There was given me a thorn in my flesh . . . Three
times I pleaded with the Lord to take it away from me.*

Paul, 2 Corinthians 12:7–8

Sometimes I wonder if the apostle Paul tried to give
tweezers to the Lord as he pleaded with Him to remove the
thorn that was tormenting him. I probably would have.

We don't know exactly what the apostle's "thorn" was—
perhaps a vision problem—but we do know that Paul was no
sissy. If he was begging, it was bad. Still, God didn't take it
away.

God answered, "My grace is sufficient to sustain you, Paul.
I'll never hold a thorn to your side without supplying enough
sweet grace to enable you to bear it." Not the answer he was
hoping for. Me either.

And Paul was a special friend of God's, an incredibly tire-
less and faithful servant. I wonder if people told him he had
sin in his life, or lacked faith?

We don't know the reason God refused to remove it any more than we know for certain what it was, or all that God accomplished through it. We do know that it was a place where God applied the ointment of His grace. And we know that it kept Paul humble and relying on the Lord for strength.

Who wants the constant stab of something that we believe is hindering our work for the Lord, maybe even threatening our life? Something that has the power to distract, humble, and waylay us? Persistent pain and problems—of whatever variety—sap energy, demand attention, and churn up doubts and fear.

I told the Lord I'd like to avoid dealing with the thorny issue of such pain, but He wouldn't let me get away with that. Because He is Truth and I am His servant. So I have to tell it like it is, even if writing about a God who deliberately holds us in a place of pain is unpopular with everyone, including me. We don't want to accept the idea of a heavenly Father who uses such a commodity. It's hard to "give away" a God like that, and sometimes hard to keep Him, too.

One of the most important and difficult tasks God has given me in life, and in my writing, is to face, and to help others face, the reality of who He is. He really is love! He really is good. And He really does deal in pain in this world. And I really don't like it.

Sometimes He removes and heals pain. Sometimes He permits and accomplishes things through it. Sometimes He even sends it. How unpopular is that last truth? When we want to avoid certain truths, we tend to label them "unscriptural." But I can't read the Scriptures without running into all three of these truths over and over. God uses this world's hurts, even though they don't originate in Him.

Pain is an arrow that Satan hurls and that God grabs, bends, and sends to His righteous purpose. But He ran it through His own heart first, so it comes dripping with the life-giving blood of His grace and love. God's purpose is that everyone should come to fully know Him, and live in His eternal love and joy in a place forever without sorrow and hurt. Not a single thorn in heaven.

What an amazing God we serve, who will use pain to get us to a place forever free of it! We don't have to understand or like the way it works. We just have to trust Him, submit to Him, and thank Him. It helps to remember the apostle Paul's words from prison, "I know that . . . what has happened to me will turn out for my deliverance" (Philippians 1:19).

We are also encouraged by Joseph's words to his brothers who had thrown him into a well and sold him into slavery in Egypt. "You intended to harm me," Joseph said, "but God intended it for good to accomplish what is now being done, the saving of many lives" (Genesis 50:20).

But it's not easy for us, any more than it is easy for our heavenly Father, when we must go through painful things.

When a parent must hold down a beloved child to receive chemotherapy or radiation, it is not so that the little one can suffer, but so that the child can live. The child can hear the parent's words, "Oh, Darling, you must go through this so you can have a chance to get well. Trust me. I know it's hard—I know it hurts—I know you hate it! I do too! But we have to go through this so you can be well and strong again. I love you so much, I can't bear to lose you. I want to keep you with me. I want you to grow up and become all you were meant to be, and do all you were meant to do—even better things than you can imagine yet. I want you to be able to get married and have your own children someday. I want you to laugh, and love, and do great things for the world. If you let me help you go through this, perhaps you can do all that someday. This won't last forever. I'm here, my dear one. I'm here. I love you so much. Hold on! It will be better one day. So much better."

The child hears the words, but doesn't fully understand. Someday, though, the child will understand, and will thank the parent for doing what was so very hard to do, bearing what was so hard to bear so that the child could live.

Someday we, too, will understand and thank our heavenly Father. It's safe to begin thanking Him now because although human cures sometimes fail, God's cure never does.

The principle of chemotherapy creates an interesting analogy for us. Chemotherapy poisons the entire system in an effort to destroy the deadly, cancerous cells. That's why it makes people so ill. The doctor must be wise and good, and the person must be strong and brave to endure this cure, which often works to make way for life in place of death. It may not be the treatment of choice if the cancer is localized, but it is often necessary when the entire system is permeated with cancer. Spot radiation won't do in this case.

This world of ours has cancer. The world's entire system has been permeated with deadly, multiplying sin. A single cancerous cell of rebellion has gone out of control, as both sin and cancer do. Sin has metastasized in this world. Only Jesus was strong enough to endure the cure for such a consuming sickness. He chose to let our sin produce death for His body. Then He produced life and healing for us as He conquered death.

This world is in its final, declining stage with sin's cancer, but God will not give up on His rescue effort. In great mercy He is increasing His effort to save His dying children. Sometimes we may have to experience some of the pain. He chose not to take us out of this world, but prayed that the Father would keep us safe within it as He uses us in His salvation plan.

If God asks me to suffer because I'm in close proximity to cancer cells that are killing His beloved children, dare I say, "Stop the treatment! This is hurting me too!"? I might want to, but I can't say that.

Dear Lord, give us grace to endure what You call us to endure for the sake of Your kingdom, no matter how much it hurts. We cannot help but love a God who gives himself to save the dying sons and daughters of Adam and Eve. *(LH)*

The Spirit himself testifies with our spirit that we are God's children. Now if we are children, then we are heirs—heirs of God and co-heirs with Christ, if indeed we share in his sufferings in order that we may also share in his glory.

I consider that our present sufferings are not worth comparing with the glory that will be revealed in us. The creation waits in eager expectation for the sons of God to be revealed. For the creation was subjected to frustration, not by its own choice, but by the will of the one who subjected it, in hope that the creation itself will be liberated from its bondage to decay and brought into the glorious freedom of the children of God.

We know that the whole creation has been groaning as in the pains of childbirth right up to the present time. Not only so, but we ourselves, who have the firstfruits of the Spirit, groan inwardly as we wait eagerly for our adoption as sons, the redemption of our bodies. For in this hope we were saved.

ROMANS 8:16–24

A Circle of Rest

Drop thy still dews of quietness
till all our striving cease.
John Greenleaf Whittier

Teach me, Lord!
I know I need to learn a lesson
of restraint,
of priorities,
or I would never be this tired.
But teach me, Father,
not from the distance of heaven
nor from behind a pulpit or podium,
but from within your embrace.
Teach me your tender love and leading
as I rest on your
mighty shoulder,
then whisper to me
what I keep forgetting . . .

I must rest within your arms
constantly
to rest within your will. *(EBP)*

Find rest, O my soul, in God alone; my hope comes from him.

PSALM 62:5

Come to me, all you who are weary and burdened, and I will give you rest. Take my yoke upon you and learn from me, for I am gentle and humble in heart, and you will find rest for your souls. For my yoke is easy and my burden is light.

JESUS, MATTHEW 11:28–30

The Bridge of Forgiveness

*He that cannot forgive others, breaks the bridge over
which he himself must pass if he would ever reach
heaven; for everyone has need to be forgiven.*

George Herbert

The potential for misuse is inherent within every bridge
of friendship. Jesus knew this all too well. He also seemed to
know that His friends would frequently wrong one another,
so He sat them down and outlined the steps for rebuilding the
bridge when one party damaged it through abuse or neglect
(Matthew 18:15–20).

He explained that the first step was for the offended
friend to point out the problem privately to the offending
friend. Hopefully that would be enough. If not, he or she
was to take two others along and try again. If that failed, the
help of the church was to be enlisted. If the person failed to
renounce his or her sin even after this extreme measure, then

and only then, the offender was to be shunned (implying that a reckless, unrepentant person is a danger to the openness required of true love).

Apparently Peter thought this sounded like a lot of trouble and got to wondering how many times he'd be required to go through such a difficult process. So he pulled Jesus aside and suggested an upper limit of seven—surely a generous number under the circumstances.

But Jesus was into "higher math" and told Peter he had to forgive his brother not "up to seven, but up to seventy times seven"! Perhaps Peter walked away astounded at the number of offenses that his brothers could inflict upon him, never realizing that Jesus may have been suggesting that he might need to forgive a brother that many times for a single serious offense.

When trust has been violated, forgiveness is seldom a one-step process, especially if the relationship is to be restored. Close friendship has a built-in vulnerability because through it we allow another person to know the best and worst that we are. When trust is broken in such a relationship, we run hard against the need to forgive, often again and again, as each new opportunity to trust presents itself. Complete forgiveness is a process that unfolds in layers of fresh affirmation.

As difficult as this is, and even though much prayer and wisdom must surround and guide us, it is only as God leads us to transparently trust once again that full healing and restoration can be brought to a relationship.

In forgiving and inclining ourselves to the repentant one who has wronged us, we follow God's amazing example. When God sent His Son to us, we disregarded, abused, and finally killed Him. Yet as we confess our sin He not only forgives us, He dares to entrust this same beloved Son to live within us!

It is this Friend who promises never to leave or forsake us (though He knows our failings and weaknesses). He is the Friend who says that if we confess our sins He will forgive our sins. It is this wonderful Friend who teaches us that when we forgive others (however many times it takes) we are merely passing along the favor of His redemptive grace. (CB)

———————— ✧ ————————

If your brother sins against you, go and show him his fault, just between the two of you. If he listens to you, you have won your brother over. But if he will not listen, take one or two others along, so that 'every matter may be established by the testimony of two or three witnesses.' If he refuses to listen to them, tell it to the church; and if he refuses to listen even to the church, treat him as you would a pagan or a tax collector.

JESUS, MATTHEW 18:15–17

Peter came to Jesus and asked, "Lord, how many times shall I forgive my brother when he sins against me? Up to seven times?" Jesus answered, "I tell you, not seven times, but seventy-seven times."

MATTHEW 18:21–22

If you forgive men [people] their trespasses, your heavenly Father also will forgive you; but if you do not forgive men [people] their trespasses, neither will your Father forgive your trespasses.

JESUS, MATTHEW 6:14–15 RSV

Bear with each other and forgive whatever grievances you may have against one another. Forgive as the Lord forgave you.

COLOSSIANS 3:13

Learning to Listen

Listen deeply to the hopes that lie
beneath our frustrations, within our
anger, or behind our depressive feeling.
David Augsburger, When Enough Is Enough

Our frustration must get frustrated with us at times. It talks and talks, trying to get our attention, trying to tell us where we're out of balance . . . where we're disorganized . . . where our priorities are not our own . . . where we're trying to prove our worth . . . where we've settled for external calm in place of internal peace . . . where we're covering or compensating for someone else's irresponsibility . . . where we're trying to be all things to all people . . . where we're chasing impossible ideals . . . and where we're tripping over our own bad habits and wrong thinking.

But too often we don't listen. We chastise our frustration as though it were the disease rather than the symptom. So it struggles on, valiantly trying to tell us why the pressure outside us has turned into stress inside us. Endlessly it whispers that our attitudes and expectations may be causing more problems than our circumstances.

And frustration may be only one of the voices clamoring for attention. Exhaustion is groaning its own suggestions. Depression and despair mutter persistent insights. And anger often shouts its declarations over the din of it all.

"How dare they expect so much of me?"

"No matter how hard I try, it's never good enough!"

"Nobody asks what I want!"

"I'll never get caught up!"

"Oh, for just one uninterrupted minute to myself!"

"Whatever I'm doing, I always feel guilty for not doing something else!"

"I can't remember when I last felt rested!"

"What's the use?"

Are we brave enough to stop maligning the messengers and listen to them instead? Faulty beliefs, unrealistic hopes, or deep needs may be revealed in such statements as those above.

Is exhaustion trying to tell us that our worth is not measured by what we produce? Is despair trying to convince us that pleasing everyone won't guarantee their love? Is disappointment trying to tell us that we can't be personally responsible for someone else's happiness? Is anger trying to convince us that conflict is sometimes necessary and good? Is fear trying to tell us that failing doesn't make us a failure? Is dissatisfaction trying to tell us that someone else may be able to do a task as well as we do it? And might frustration itself be reminding us that trying harder won't create a perfect life?

It won't always be pleasant to let the Lord search our hearts and teach us through the voice of our own need. But if we listen carefully we can work with Him to set new, realistic priorities. The actions that result will bring rest and balance to our lives. He knows us and longs to bring us peace. We are safe with Him. (EBP)

The lamp of the Lord searches the spirit of a man; it searches out his inmost being.

PROVERBS 20:27

O Lord, you have searched me and you know me. You know when I sit and when I rise; you perceive my thoughts from afar. You discern my going out and my lying down; you are familiar with all my ways. Before a word is on my tongue you know it completely, O Lord. You hem me in—behind and before; you have laid your hand upon me. Such knowledge is too wonderful for me, too lofty for me to attain. Where can I go from your Spirit? Where can I flee from your presence? . . . Search me, O God, and know my heart; test me and know my anxious thoughts.

See if there is any offensive way in me and lead me in the way everlasting.

PSALM 139:1–7, 23–24

Walking While Waiting

With your help I can advance.
David, 2 Samuel 22:30

*S*ometimes we are certain that we're going nowhere in life. We are trapped between the walls of some narrow, spartan place that we're sure must be one of life's dreary waiting rooms. So we sit down, reach for an outdated periodical, and wait for someone to open a door and call our name.

Many of us who think we are being patient may actually be camping out in one of life's hallways! Our Lord's house has many rooms, and how can we get from one to another except through a hallway? Yes, some are long, some narrow, some dark, and some cold. Yet if we fail to understand the purpose of a hallway, we're likely to wander about for years, assuming we are "waiting on the Lord."

Life's hallways *are* places of transition even though we see no change. And because God is with us, such places offer our finest progress.

When faith holds out a hand to God in the dark, we're already *there* even though we haven't yet *arrived*. Waiting on God is the same as walking with God toward exciting new rooms of potential and service.

But we can't see progress in a dark hallway. And although we don't like being stuck there without a flashlight, few other places are so quiet and devoid of outside distractions.

Windowless halls can be the perfect place to discover God and His quiet grace. They are places where time seems to stand still and so we stop and give names to our deepest needs and then give them up to God's care and timing.

On days when we're feeling tired or hopelessly lost, He carries us in His arms. At other times He waits until we grope for His hand and begin to follow along, learning to walk by *faith*, not by *sight*.

When we finally arrive at the door that swings open into the light, we realize that our heavenly Father can see perfectly well in the dark. We can trust Him to bring us to the next door in His perfect time—the time that will most benefit us and the glory of His name.

Let's practice waiting on the Lord, even as we faithfully walk the narrow way. *(NR)*

Let your eyes look straight ahead, fix your gaze directly before you. Make level paths for your feet and take only

ways that are firm. Do not swerve to the right or the left;
keep your foot from evil.

PROVERBS 4:25–27

But one thing I do: Forgetting what is behind and strain-
ing toward what is ahead, I press on toward the goal to
win the prize for which God has called me heavenward in
Christ Jesus. All of us who are mature should take such
a view of things.

PHILIPPIANS 3:13–15

Rejoice in the Lord always. I will say it again: Rejoice! Let
your gentleness be evident to all. The Lord is near. Do not
be anxious about anything, but in everything, by prayer and
petition, with thanksgiving, present your requests to God.
And the peace of God, which transcends all understanding,
will guard your hearts and your minds in Christ Jesus . . .
For I have learned to be content whatever the circumstances
. . . I can do everything through him who gives me strength.

PHILIPPIANS 4:4–7, 11, 13

You are my lamp, O Lord; the Lord turns my darkness
into light . . . It is God who arms me with strength and
makes my way perfect . . . You broaden the path beneath
me, so that my ankles do not turn.

2 SAMUEL 22:29, 33, 37

What a Name!

A name, when used in the Bible, is not merely a designation; it is a definition. God's names reveal certain characteristics which are disclosed only when His people enter an area of special need.

Selwyn Hughes

You wrote your glorious name
  across the heavens and it read
    Elohim—The Creator.
You pronounced your holy name
  to your people and it was
    Yahweh—Lord of Relationship.
You posted your powerful name
  at life's valleys and dead ends and it was
    El Shaddai—All Sufficient God.
You spoke your lovely name
  into fears and conflicts and it was
    Jehovah Shalom—The Lord Our Peace.
You whispered your compassionate name

into sorrow and brokenness and it was
Jehovah Jireh—The Lord Provides.
You signed your most beautiful name
in blood upon our hearts and it was
Jesus—Jehovah is Salvation. *(LH)*

Let them praise your great and awesome name.

PSALM 99:3

The name of the Lord is a strong tower; the righteous run to it and are safe.

PROVERBS 18:10

Everyone who calls on the name of the Lord will be saved.

ACTS 2:21

Therefore God exalted him to the highest place and gave him the name that is above every name, that at the name of Jesus every knee should bow, in heaven and on earth and under the earth, and every tongue confess that Jesus Christ is Lord, to the glory of God the Father.

PHILIPPIANS 2:9–11

Let the name of the Lord be praised, both now and forevermore. From the rising of the sun to the place where it sets, the name of the Lord is to be praised. The Lord is

exalted over all the nations, his glory above the heavens.
Who is like the Lord our God, the One who sits enthroned
on high, who stoops down to look on the heavens and the
earth? He raises the poor from the dust and lifts the needy
from the ash heap; he seats them with princes, with the
princes of their people. He settles the barren woman in
her home as a happy mother of children. Praise the Lord.

PSALM 113:2–9

Rejoice, My Soul!

**Bring joy to your servant, for to
you, O Lord, I lift up my soul.**
King David, Psalm 86:4

I love the way the psalmist would have heart-to-heart talks with himself—especially when he was upset about something.

Can't you almost see David tugging his shirt open with both hands, lowering his chin into his collar and saying, "Hey, down there! What's your problem? Why are you so disturbed? Where did all your joy go?"

I don't know if his soul actually answered him or not, but he often proceeded to ask a lot of questions or make a lot of statements designed to change his emotional and spiritual landscape. He seemed to know how to work his way back to the joy every time it deserted him. We would do well to take lessons at his feet, because joy is as essential to us as air and water.

Joy is our eternal birthright as God's dearly loved children, and He means for it to begin now. Joy is life's bubbles, its song, and often its medicine. Joy knows how to lift our burdens and carry us over the rough spots in life.

And the joy of the Lord cannot, we soon discover, be kept cooped up inside us. It much prefers to come out to play in laughter, smiles, songs, dancing, praise, and endless kind words and actions. Soon joy becomes a "people magnet," drawing others into its warmth and light. God's joy is a party—a banquet—and everyone is invited.

Joy is our soul expressing its wonder in who and what God is, and joy increases as He increases. Joy is the dance of the redeemed. Joy is life, speaking back to Life, our gratitude.

Joy shouts to my soul, "Go ahead and dance on the dungheap; you already know the outcome! You've already sampled the eternal good fruit God grows from this world's fertilizer. So go ahead and trust! Sing! Dance in the midst!"

But mired feet can't dance. Joy is difficult to find in the muck. Sometimes life even suggests that joy is inappropriate. And when we do find it, we can't always keep it. This world's thorns poke holes in our fragile containers, allowing our joy to leak.

When this happened to David, he acknowledged the problem, and then set about addressing it within himself. He didn't pretend that if he were a truly godly man, or a truly successful servant of the Most High God, he would never feel upset, frightened, discouraged, deserted, ashamed, or depressed. He never pretended that he was experiencing joy when he wasn't. He simply asked himself what had taken the place of his joy, and began dealing with it.

He reminded himself of God's great love and goodness. He revived his perspective, renewed his trust, rekindled his hope, restored his relationship, and ultimately received once more the joy of the Lord. I especially love the way he then spread it around, inviting every living thing in heaven and on earth to join in the party of praise.

You and I also have the privilege of inviting men and angels to rejoice. But first we need to invite our own soul to sing. *(LH)*

Why are you downcast, O my soul? Why so disturbed within me? Put your hope in God, for I will yet praise him, my Savior and my God. My soul is downcast within me; therefore I will remember you.

PSALM 42:5–6

Find rest, O my soul, in God alone; my hope comes from him. He alone is my rock and my salvation; he is my fortress, I will not be shaken.

PSALM 62:5–6

When anxiety was great within me, your consolation brought joy to my soul.

PSALM 94:19

Praise the Lord, O my soul; all my inmost being, praise his holy name. Praise the Lord, O my soul, and forget not all his benefits—who forgives all your sins and heals all your diseases, who redeems your life from the pit and crowns you with love and compassion, who satisfies your desires with good things so that your youth is renewed like the eagle's . . .

Praise the Lord, you his angels, you mighty ones who do his bidding, who obey his word. Praise the Lord, all his heavenly hosts, you his servants who do his will. Praise the Lord, all his works everywhere in his dominion. Praise the Lord, O my soul.

PSALM 103:1–5, 20–22

What Did I Expect?

A real friend has no strings, no binding
preconceptions, no limiting agendas . . .
The bond of love releases people.
Lloyd John Ogilvie

If we dared to unwrap and examine the feelings we have for those closest to us, I suspect that many of us would find a somewhat mixed package. Not only do we cherish our loved ones for who and what they are, but also for what we need them to be.

This hidden "wish list" affects our relationships with family members, friends, and, probably most often, the one to whom we are married.

Unacknowledged and unexplored expectations can frustrate, disappoint, and tie us in knots. They prove to be even more frustrating to the person who fails to match our dreams.

Most of us have not consciously entered our close relationships with preconceived notions. Yet each of us has grown up with a unique set of hopes, fears, and perceptions that have shaped our longing for the "ideal friend" or "perfect partner." Such desires and aspirations may have created a natural affinity for the heart of a particular kind of person, leading us toward our choice of friends or mate.

Inevitably, these people prove to be who they are, not who we thought they were or who we wanted them to be. Our level of frustration and disappointment reveals our hidden expectations. In healthy relationships we share our hearts and lives, but sometimes we forget that we cannot expect another person to fix our brokenness or fill in where someone else failed us. Sometimes the wishful heart forgets that no one outside of Christ can meet all of our needs or fulfill all of our hopes for security, love, perfect understanding, and unfailing loyalty.

Occasionally we even discover that we have written our own hidden definitions of how love should prove itself. Our expectations scrawl deep longings in a language read constantly by the fingertips of our feelings—assessing, measuring, evaluating. "If she cared she wouldn't be so busy . . ." "If he loved me he would know how I feel . . ." "If she were a real friend she'd call more often . . ." or "he'd buy me gifts . . ." or "she wouldn't criticize me . . ." or "he'd always ask how my day went."

Such assumptions don't always voice themselves. They are reoccurring feelings of neglect, disappointment, or disapproval that create great unhappiness for us.

And when we allow our expectations to define the worthiness of our loved one, we create great unhappiness for him or her. If he doesn't understand or express his emotions like I do, then clearly, something is wrong with him. Since she doesn't think or act the way I do, she's not just different, she's deficient. We may even begin to manipulate others, seeking to change them into people who are better suited to meet our needs.

Yet if we are to be good, true, and righteous friends, we will not seek to refashion one another to meet our expectations. We will be careful not to accept one another with only our heads and our mouths, while nourishing disapproval in our hearts.

Instead, each of us will loose our dreads and dreams in open sharing. We will speak our needs, content to let them rest lightly in the hand and heart of our loved one. Then we will see what God and we can do, together.

I expect great things of honest friends. (CB)

Teach me your way, O Lord, and I will walk in your truth; give me an undivided heart.

PSALM 86:11

The wisdom of the prudent is to give thought to their ways.

PROVERBS 14:8

All a man's [woman's] ways seem right to him [her], but the Lord weighs the heart.

PROVERBS 21:2

Search me, O God, and know my heart; test me and know my anxious thoughts. See if there is any offensive way in me, and lead me in the way everlasting.

PSALM 139:23–24

So from now on we regard no one from a worldly point of view . . . Therefore, if anyone is in Christ, he is a new creation; the old has gone, the new has come! All this is from God, who reconciled us to himself through Christ and gave us the ministry of reconciliation.

2 CORINTHIANS 5:16–18

Where the Spirit of the Lord is, there is freedom.

2 CORINTHIANS 3:17

Life's Confusing Caves

Sometimes a cave is God's corridor to the future.

You can't figure out what's going on. Everywhere you go and everything you do seems to deliver nothing but pressure and pain. You're not harboring unconfessed sin in your life, or creating your own problems with foolish choices, so what's happening?

You desperately hang onto the truth that God is good and delivers what He promises. Yet where are the promised blessings? Where are the victories? Why has God been permitting people and circumstances to harass and hem you in like this? You just want to run away and hide.

Join David in the cave of Adullam, the dark hiding place of a man who was promised a throne but was crowned with nothing but problems. No throne in sight.

One might logically assume that when God places a specific call on a person's life, that person would not be left to wait and wonder and wander around for years, struggling with circumstances that lead everywhere else. But that's exactly what happened to David. (See 1 Samuel 16–31 for the whole story.)

Several miserable years had passed since this surprised young man had been called in from the field, where he was contentedly tending his father's sheep, to face the prophet Samuel. Samuel pronounced that God had chosen David to replace Saul as king of Israel, and he promptly anointed the young boy with oil. Wow! Time to trade in his field clothes for royal robes.

Not quite. He entered the palace scene with a harp, not a scepter. Court musician. The songs he'd written under the stars to calm restless sheep were now needed to sooth the agitated and tormented King Saul.

Other kingly duties? Slingshot detail. With a stone and his trusty slingshot, he felled a nine-foot giant named Goliath, who had been intimidating the entire army of Israel. David went to war, racking up huge military victories as he repeatedly slaughtered thousands of Israel's enemies. A blood-soaked battlefield instead of a palace?

In payment, the insecure and jealous king decided that his faithful servant was a threat to him, so he began trying to kill him. David had to run for his life. He ended up in the Philistine town of Gath, not the safest place for him since he had killed his share of Philistines in his military endeavors. Someone recognized him, and to save his own life, David had to carry on like a madman, pawing on the gates and letting saliva run down his beard.

This is when David escaped to the cave of Adullam, spit drying in his beard, undoubtedly confused, and desperately in need of someone to comfort him. So who does God send to his cave?

His brothers! Those same sweet siblings who mocked him at the battlefront when he stepped forward to slay Goliath. "Why have you come down here?" his oldest brother had asked haughtily. "And with whom did you leave those few sheep in the desert? I know how conceited you are and how wicked your heart is; you came down only to watch the battle" (1 Samuel 17:28).

Nice family. So glad to have you in my cave.

Next David is joined by hundreds of society's distressed, debt-ridden, and discontented. Not exactly the kind of company I hope for when I run away.

In addition to all of this, David was trying to find a safe place for his aging mother and father to stay during his cave tenure. He really needed to get them taken care of because he didn't know "what God would do for [him]" (1 Samuel 22:3). Small wonder that he wondered—this anointed king whose throne was a stone, whose palace was a cave, and whose kingdom was a gang of society's disgruntled rejects.

So why this miserable cave scene? Was David being punished for something? Had he made some wrong choices? Did he have a bad attitude? There's nothing in his life so far to suggest that this was so.

There's everything to suggest that the fulfillment of God's highest and best promises come at the end of a path of pain. Perhaps it is the pain that prepares and purifies us. No one wants to believe that this is God's way. We don't want to remember that it was the cross and the cave—Christ's temporary grave—that led the way to resurrection and eternal, abundant life.

We prefer to blame it all on the enemy. We whine as if the devil has gotten by with some sneak attack when God wasn't looking. Or else we blame it on that poor person who is already suffering, who "must be doing something wrong or she wouldn't be going through all this."

We forget that Jesus promised we would have trouble in this world. In fact, He said that we *may* have peace—a choice, an available possibility—but we *will* have trouble—no choice, an absolute certainty (John 16:33). Yes, sometimes we'll have trouble even when we're doing what's right. He asked us to take heart in the fact that He has overcome the world. He is practiced at turning the enemy's tricks to His own good purposes.

But while God works things out, we might find it necessary to "hide away for awhile." Escape or protection is sometimes appropriate, as it was for David in the cave of Adullam.

Yet even then, we may find God allowing what looks like more trouble to follow us into our caves. This may well become the stuff of our strength. Those four hundred malcontents who gathered with David became the power base that would sustain him throughout his later years as king—his most faithful men. Had he rejected them as just another unwelcome stress in his life, he would have missed the beginning of God's blessing for him. He went into the cave alone, but he came out leading warriors.

We use our cave times to rest—to learn—to grow—to prepare—to receive all that God has for us. So even if life doesn't get better, we get better at living it. Take heart. We will yet reign with Him! *(LH)*

Your granite cave a hiding place,
your high cliff aerie a place of safety.
You're my cave to hide in,
my cliff to climb.
Be my safe leader,
be my true mountain guide.
Free me from hidden traps;
I want to hide in you.
I've put my life in your hands.
You won't drop me,
you'll never let me down.

PSALM 31:2–5 *The Message*

Have mercy on me, O God, have mercy on me, for in you my soul takes refuge. I will take refuge in the shadow of your wings until the disaster has passed.

81

I cry out to God Most High, to God, who fulfills his purpose for me. He sends from heaven and saves me, rebuking those who hotly pursue me; God sends his love and his faithfulness.

I am in the midst of lions; I lie among ravenous beasts—men whose teeth are spears and arrows, whose tongues are sharp swords.

Be exalted, O God, above the heavens; let your glory be over all the earth.

They spread a net for my feet—I was bowed down in distress. They dug a pit in my path—but they have fallen into it themselves.

My heart is steadfast, O God, my heart is steadfast; I will sing and make music. Awake, my soul! Awake, harp and lyre! I will awaken the dawn.

I will praise you, O Lord, among the nations; I will sing of you among the peoples. For great is your love, reaching to the heavens; your faithfulness reaches to the skies.

Be exalted, O God, above the heavens; let your glory be over all the earth.

DAVID, FROM THE CAVE WHERE HE
FLED FROM SAUL, PSALM 57:1–11

Treasures of Darkness

Ye fearful saints, fresh courage take, the clouds ye so much dread are big with mercy, and shall break in blessings on your head.

William Cowper

Within the depths of
His darkest clouds
God often seems to bury His
richest treasures—
    silver streaks of growth,
    sterling faith,
    precious, gleaming truths—
for His beloved children.
Has a dense cloud of
    doubt,
    pain,
    loss,
    trouble,
    frustration, or
    loneliness

settled over you, dear one?
Search out the treasures of darkness!
The riches of your heavenly Father hide there—
with your name engraved in silver! *(NR)*

I will give you the treasures of darkness, riches stored in secret places, so that you may know that I am the Lord, the God of Israel, who summons you by name.

ISAIAH 45:3

From now on I will tell you of new things, of hidden things unknown to you. They are created now, and not long ago; you have not heard of them before today.

ISAIAH 48:6–7

I am the Lord, and there is no other; apart from me there is no God. I will strengthen you, though you have not acknowledged me, so that from the rising of the sun to the place of its setting men may know there is none besides me. I am the Lord, and there is no other. I form the light and create darkness, I bring prosperity and create disaster; I, the Lord, do all these things . . . Turn to me and be saved, all you ends of the earth; for I am God, and there is no other . . . They will say of me, "In the Lord alone are righteousness and strength."

ISAIAH 45:5–7, 22, 24

Multiplied Sorrows

*I add to my troubles when I treat myself
even worse than my loss is treating me.*

*L*eft to itself, life does a fair amount of dividing and sub-
tracting. Death and distance divide. Divorce and disagreement divide. Many treasured things are subtracted from our
lives by decay, disease, deception, desertion, depravity, and
the other effects of sin in this world. In spite of our best ef-
forts, we often find ourselves on the losing end of life.

So why do we add to our own sorrows?

Subconsciously, we compare ourselves to someone who
is better off, and we feel worse. Or we blame ourselves for
doing what we did or for not doing what we should have
done or could have done. The "if onlys" set up headquarters
in our hearts. Anger boils until it hardens into resentment,
bitterness, and unforgiveness. We jump to conclusions, feed
negative thoughts, make assumptions, anticipate and predict
the worst. And we bombard ourselves with an endless volley
of depressing messages:

- I can't survive or even be happy again without this thing/person.
- I will never get through this.
- I must be a failure/bad/hopeless.
- The rest of my life is going to be miserable.
- I have been singled out for abuse.
- I will always feel this afraid/vulnerable/angry/depressed.
- God has deserted me.
- I can't make it through one more night.
- No one can help.

If we catch ourselves in the act of saying, doing, or believing such things, we have an opportunity to tell ourselves the truth instead.

- Yes I hurt, but I will not hurt forever.
- Even pain has a beginning, a middle, and an end.
- I will survive.
- God does care.
- Some of God's people know how to comfort me.
- Even if this is my fault, beating myself won't help.
- God loves me tenderly when I'm hurting.
- I can't see it through these tears, but God does have a future for me.
- Morning will come. (WLT)

Let the wise listen and add to their learning.

PROVERBS 1:5

Each of you must put off falsehood and speak truthfully.

EPHESIANS 4:25

Do not add to what I command you and do not subtract from it.

DEUTERONOMY 4:2

Now may the Lord of peace himself give you peace at all times and in every way.

2 THESSALONIANS 3:16

The Shape of a Question

*God is more concerned about what is
happening in me than is happening to me.*

Gordon R. Bear

*L*ife wasn't going the way it was supposed to go. Its con-
tinuing trouble and heartache were weighing me down with a
leaden "why"-shaped question mark that wound itself around
my neck. I took the question to my husband, hoping for an
answer. He had none.

Of all my wise and wonderful friends, at least three can
be counted on for an insightful opinion on nearly any subject, especially if asked. I asked. Not only did they have no
opinion, they had no clues. One friend, the one I was positive
would have some sort of an answer whether I liked it or not,
said, "I'm as puzzled as you are about this."

Another friend listened as my long string of recent losses
shaped itself into the giant question mark. Then she heard

me stab the point at its end as I cried out, "What is God trying to tell me with all of this?"

"I'm afraid I have no answer for that," she said gently, "but may I pray for you?" And she did, right there on the phone.

It wasn't long after her loving prayer that I began to understand a rule about questioning God. If I'm asking and not seeming to get an answer, perhaps I'm asking the wrong question. Maybe it needs to be rephrased—or redirected.

My question needed both. And when I gave it some room to maneuver, I found it deliberately curving back at me and rephrasing itself. It no longer asked, "What is God trying to tell me?" Instead it asked, "What have I been telling God by my reaction?" Perhaps I've been telling Him that I don't trust Him. That I don't believe He's in control. That He's not the giver of good gifts. Or that He doesn't really have my best interest at heart.

And then the question mark relaxed its crooked posture and reformed itself into a very straight, very confident, very pointed exclamation mark. My own attitude was the problem!

It was time to put away the childish measuring stick that uses circumstances to measure the love and character of God. It was time to reaffirm the truth that God is good, holy, just, sovereign, wise, and that He is Love—pure and beautiful. So I deliberately stopped asking "why" and "what" and began to ask "how."

"How, Lord, are You going to bring good for me and glory for You out of all of this?"

I'm so glad that God's results are not limited by His raw materials! I am waiting and watching. I love the way He works—first in me, then *around* me. (WLT)

Therefore, my dear friends . . . continue to work out your salvation with fear and trembling, for it is God who works in you to will and to act according to his good purpose.

PHILIPPIANS 2:12–13

Dear friends, don't be bewildered or surprised when you go through the fiery trials ahead, for this is no strange, unusual thing that is going to happen to you. Instead, be really glad—because these trials will make you partners with Christ in his suffering, and afterwards you will have the wonderful joy of sharing his glory in that coming day when it will be displayed . . . So if you are suffering according to God's will, keep on doing what is right and trust yourself to the God who made you, for he will never fail you.

1 PETER 4:12–13, 19 TLB

This Isn't Funny Anymore

> *The workshop of character is everyday life.*
> **Maltbie D. Babcock**

The four of us stood in the blazing sun and sagebrush and roadside dust watching our car spew forth its heated opinion about our forcing it to climb mountain roads at its age. Any hope of making it to our niece's wedding on time seemed to be going up in smoke too.

My husband, Herb, and our officially ASE certified "World Class Auto Technician" son, Jeff, wore the look men wear when they know exactly what's happening but can't do a thing about it. My daughter-in-law, Margie, and I wore the look women wear when they see their husbands look like that but can't do a thing about it.

Herb was supposed to be videotaping the wedding. Margie had agreed to coordinate the proceedings. I had promised to help my sister with last-minute details. And Jeff was to be one of the groomsmen; yet there he stood in shorts and sandals, poking around under the hood, making solemn pronouncements. "Looks like cooling system vapor lock. This car's going to need considerable time to cool off, a gallon or two of water, and some serious attention later."

We could have used a similar prescription. This wasn't just a bad day we were having, it was a "last straw" day. A sense of humor seemed way beyond my emotional reach, so I settled for a sense of balance.

"Just don't make things worse," I kept saying to myself. "Remain calm. If you can't say something good, try to focus on what needs to be done." So, as cars and trucks zoomed by, intent on reaching their destination, I stood by the car, its hood raised like a huge flag, and prayed for a solution.

Finally a knight in a shining white pickup truck pulled over and offered assistance. He left with our name, location, and my sister's phone number, promising to call for help as soon as he reached town. At least she would know what had happened to us.

Several minutes later my brother and his family, on their way to the ceremony, rescued us in time to intercept the man my sister had dispatched after hearing of our plight.

At the wedding site we stuffed our unhappy bodies into suits and ties, dresses and panty hose. We weren't the only ones feeling the heat, for the plea came, "Could you please take ice water to the thirsty bridal party?"

Thankful that I had arrived in time to help a little, I hurried to gather a pitcher of water and cups. Hands full, I kicked the screen door open only to have it slam back into the pitcher, sending a cascade of water down my face and dress. They drank what was left, I dried what I could.

In spite of delays, the wedding commenced. The bride was radiant, the groom nervous and tender, the minister (the bride's step-father) touching and genuine in his expressions of his love for them and for God. I passed tissues to my sister, my daughter, and my daughter-in-law. It's good to have experience in these matters.

After the reception, the guys headed down the mountain. They watered the car and talked severely to it, but, unheeding, it stranded us again on the way home—this time in a desolate patch of freeway between someplace and someplace else. Our daughter and son-in-law were following us, however, so at least we had help available.

On the way to the gas station, the girls bubbled with annoying good cheer. This was a family adventure, they said. We were making a memory that we would surely talk and laugh about later.

They found a huge white enameled cooking pot in the trunk of our daughter's car and filled it with water for the radiator.

Herb rode in the passenger seat dangling the pot from his thumbs, solemnly explaining (as engineers tend to do) that he was demonstrating the highly effective "decoupling theory" to prevent sloshing and spills.

The girls were certain that this was fun.

I was certain that we didn't need this much fun.

I was tired. Exhausted, really. And nothing was very funny. The day had topped off a bad week, which had followed an even worse one, after an unbelievable month that pretty much matched the whole year.

When life's heavy storms come like that, one after another, you can find yourself reeling, staggering, going to your knees, adjusting, being knocked flat again, and then struggling up in time to catch yet another blow.

The accumulated losses can become so overwhelming that it takes only the sprinkles of life's daily problems to tip your boat. Every distress feels like a disaster. Nothing looks like a simple aggravation that could, with a little perspective and humor, be turned into an adventure.

When I've lost my sense of humor, when I can no longer bend and flex with the day's stresses and distresses, I don't need to give my day or my attitude over to the Lord. I need to give myself to Him. If I hope to grow through life's sprinkles as well as its downpours, if I want to learn patience and perseverance and gain heavenly perspective, I need to hide in Him. Rest in Him. Find myself renewed in Him. He waits with healing in His wings. *(NR)*

Yet the Lord longs to be gracious to you; he rises to show you compassion. For the Lord is a God of justice. Blessed are all who wait for him! . . . How gracious he will be when you cry for help! As soon as he hears, he will answer you. Although the Lord gives you the bread of adversity, and the water of affliction, your teachers will be hidden no more; with your own eyes you will see them. Whether you turn to the right or to the left, your ears will hear a voice behind you, saying, "This is the way, walk in it." . . . He will also send you rain for the seed you sow in the ground, and the food that comes from the land will be rich and plentiful.

ISAIAH 30:18–21, 23

For you who fear my name, the Sun of Righteousness will rise with healing in his wings. And you will go free, leaping with joy like calves let out to pasture.

MALACHI 4:2 TLB

Five Ways to Handle Fear and Worry

Worry does not empty tomorrow of its sorrow, it empties today of its strength.
Corrie ten Boom

I once knew someone so
simpleminded and unaware
that fear never entered her world.
Worry never invaded her innocence.
Ignorance became bliss.

I once knew someone so
informed and educated
that future fears stalked her world.
Worry endlessly postulated doom.
Intelligence became dread.

I once knew someone so
idealistic and spiritual
that fear was denied.
Worry disguised itself as repetitious prayers.
Ideology became escapism.

I once knew someone so
capable and determined
that fear was a challenge to avoid disaster.
Worry simply required more work.
Intervention became exhaustion.

I once knew someone so
realistic and wise
that she feared and trusted only God.
This world's worries were placed in His hands.
Inability became peace. *(NR)*

[Jesus] asked them, "Why were you so fearful? Don't you
even yet have confidence in me?"

MARK 4:40 TLB

I tell you, my friends, do not be afraid of those who kill the
body and after that can do no more. But I will show you
whom you should fear: Fear him who, after the killing of

the body, has the power to throw you into hell. Yes, I tell you, fear him. Are not five sparrows sold for two pennies? Yet not one of them is forgotten by God. Indeed, the very hairs of your head are all numbered. Don't be afraid; you are worth more than many sparrows.

JESUS, LUKE 12:4–7

There is no fear in love. But perfect love drives out fear, because fear has to do with punishment. The one who fears is not made perfect in love. We love because he first loved us.

1 JOHN 4:18–19

Cast all your anxiety on him because he cares for you.

1 PETER 5:7

God has said, "Never will I leave you; never will I forsake you." So we say with confidence, "The Lord is my helper; I will not be afraid. What can man do to me?"

HEBREWS 13:5–6

The Gift of Laughter

I believe that laughter is a sacred sound to our God.
Tim Hansel, You Gotta Keep Dancin'

Not all laughter comes easily. There is a laughter that waits to be born. It is laughter at the end of exhaustion . . . laughter after pain . . . laughter for the joy of release . . . earned laughter . . . laughter all the brighter for its stark background . . . laughter stitched together with that ragged yet tough filament we call faith (or is it endurance?) . . . laughter that knows every note in the scale of life by heart—all its highs and lows—yet sings out its lilting tune anyway.

This laughter is more than just a sound, more than mirth, more than any comedian has ever hoped to evoke. It is the soul bubbling over with hope and victory. It is the voice of joy. Like a magnet it draws every scrap of life within its radius toward the promise of living, loving, and trusting.

Life does demand that we cry—often. But we need to laugh still more often. Because there will be an end to our tears, but never to our joy! *(WLT)*

There is a time for everything, and a season for every activity under heaven: . . . a time to weep and a time to laugh, a time to mourn and a time to dance.

ECCLESIASTES 3:1, 4

Blessed are you who weep now, for you will laugh.

JESUS, LUKE 6:21

Those who sow in tears will reap with songs of joy. He [she] who goes out weeping, carrying seed to sow, will return with songs of joy, carrying sheaves with him [her].

PSALM 126:5–6

Who's Hurting Now?

Jesus,
I'll know who's
number one
if I count the
tears.
Have I shed more
for your grief,
or mine?

When life is difficult, we might try setting aside our own pain and asking God what hurts Him. Does it hurt Him when He shows us the beauty of His light and we turn away toward darkness? When He fits us with the spectacles of His heavenly view and we grope myopically? When He offers uncommon guidance and we follow our own common sense? When He shows us *the* Way and we are content to take *any old* way?

Do His eyes get misty when He spreads a banquet of love before us and we pass it up to nibble on the dry crumbs of hate and resentment? When He offers power to move mountains and we stumble over dirt clods? When He delivers us from evil and we wink at His Enemy? When we cling to Him in pain and then wave to Him in ease? When He presents peace and we battle over it? When He offers salvation to all and we hoard it as a private joy? When we cry out to Him to save us but refuse to live in the safety of His presence?

He waits to help in our weakness, sin, and failure. He already shared *our* pain. When we begin to understand His pain, growth begins. (*WLT*)

"For my thoughts are not your thoughts, neither are your ways my ways," declares the Lord. "As the heavens are higher than the earth, so are my ways higher than your ways and my thoughts than your thoughts."

ISAIAH 55:8–9

God looks down from heaven on the sons [and daughters] of men to see if there are any who understand, any who seek God . . . Will the evildoers never learn—those who . . . do not call on God? There they were, overwhelmed with dread, where there was nothing to dread.

PSALM 53:2, 4–5

Teach me your way, O Lord, and I will walk in your truth; give me an undivided heart, that I may fear your name. I will praise you, O Lord my God, with all my heart; I will glorify your name forever. For great is your love toward me.

PSALM 86:11–13

I will instruct you and teach you in the way you should go; I will counsel you and watch over you. Do not be like the horse or the mule, which have no understanding but must be controlled by bit and bridle or they will not come to you. Many are the woes of the wicked, but the Lord's unfailing love surrounds the man [woman] who trusts in him. Rejoice in the Lord and be glad, you righteous; sing, all you who are upright in heart!

PSALM 32:8–11

"Your fruitfulness comes from me." Who is wise? He will realize these things. Who is discerning? He will understand them. The ways of the Lord are right; the righteous walk in them, but the rebellious stumble in them.

HOSEA 14:8–9

Deflated Dreams

*Nothing wounds us more deeply than running
from the truth, even when truth hurts.*

Some people have a lot of wrinkled little rubber balloons of "expectations" and "hopes" lying around inside of them. They fear and avoid these deflated dreams, as though honest acknowledgment might inflate them until they explode.

Honestly facing life's disappointments can be painful. It can even seem like the ultimate disappointment. We would rather believe that if we don't look at or admit the truth, then maybe it's not real, or it doesn't matter so much after all.

"How can I admit that life stinks? That it's not turning out right? That the very people and things I most wanted to be proud of—had the highest dreams and hopes for—have deeply disappointed me? That the grand plan I had for life has been derailed? That even some of the goals that I did reach are lying on the floor too, empty of the satisfaction I thought they would bring? Why would I admit this? It sounds like an invitation to depression to me!"

No, it's an invitation to avoid depression. Buried feelings of disappointment gang up inside us and whisper lies in the dark about who we are, whose fault it is, or what the future holds. Buried disappointments believe the lies of fear and failure, and avoid the truth that would set us free. Disappointments that are brought into God's light meet His hope and resurrection power.

I think the enemy takes advantage of these hopes, dreams, and intentions that have fallen short or just exploded. I think he tries to apply them to the hope that we have in God, causing us to begin to lower our expectations of God, transferring the reality of a life that disappoints on some levels, to a God that disappoints on some levels.

But it's not God's fault. Sometimes I think about how disappointed our heavenly Father must be in the choices of His children. Parents who watch their own children make harmful choices that divert them from the path to becoming all they could be, can relate to what our Lord must be feeling.

If you are a parent grieving for your child who seems lost and derailed from God's highest intentions, know that the Father enters into your disappointment with you. He will share with that deepest aching part of your "Mother or Father heart" the reality and joy that He has not given up hope; therefore you must not either. Because He "knows himself"— He knows who He is, and what He can do. He knows the powerful resources of His great love. If He can give life to the dead, He can surely give abundant, purposeful life to the living.

Our heavenly Father truly knows all that we could be, should be, and were created to be. He doesn't know this as some vague "hope" but as reality. How it must have hurt Him to give up this reality for the lie we bought! Oh, the high intentions He had, and has, for us! Yet here we are, charting our own course and trying to pretend it doesn't matter that we aren't getting there.

Still, God enters into our "lousy choice situations" and continues giving in order to help us survive and grow in the midst of it. He longs and waits for us to become who and what He intended. Yet many of us take advantage of His grace, love, and patience for our own selfish and shortsighted gain, rather than take advantage of His grace and love to become like Him in selfless, sacrificial love. Selfishness and blindness run deep in our fallen, human condition.

Courage, dear one! God simply ain't done yet! The final chapter hasn't been written. Well, it's actually written, but we just haven't read it yet. Maybe faith and hope mean nothing more than peeking at the end of the book—reading the invisible pages through passages like 2 Corinthians 4:16–18, and Romans 8:15–39, and then getting excited and living in gratitude and joy about what He's doing. No matter what it looks like right now.

But I think this comes about only when we look at the pain honestly and weep over it. Sometimes I think we have to get the tears out to make more room for the hope and joy.

You'll know you've traded in your disappointments and deflated dreams for faith and hope when you find yourself being filled with the knowledge that God will yet change hearts and open blind eyes. And you'll really know that faith is afloat when you catch yourself praying that your child, spouse, or friend won't kick his or her backside all the way through the front-side in regret for not "getting it" sooner!

Keep loving, dear one. Keep hoping in God. I believe in Him, and I believe in you. *(LH)*

May the God of hope fill you with all joy and peace as you trust in him, so that you may overflow with hope by the power of the Holy Spirit.

ROMANS 15:13

Trust

**Blessed is the man who trusts in the
Lord, whose trust is the Lord.**
Jeremiah 17:7 RSV

Stoop-shouldered,
foot-dragging,
sighing
resignation
is not trust.
Real trust
bounces on eager toes of
anticipation—
laughs with the pure delight
of knowing
in whom it believes—
rests easy
knowing
on whom it waits.
Lord,

so wrap me in the
knowledge of You
that my trust is no longer
in You, but
is You.

Children are cutest when no one's watching—or they think no one is.

I had just stepped into the kitchen with an armload of laundry when the sight of our boys standing together on the back step caught my eye. Their backs were turned, so they didn't see me looking as the little one wrapped his arm around his brother's knees and tilted his blond head back, gazing up. He barely reached his brother's belt loops.

In a tiny voice he said, "Bend your ear down a minute—I want to tell you a secret."

Then, very quietly, he whispered something that delighted them both.

You know, Jesus, I can't help thinking as I watch them . . . after all these years of walking with You, I still don't even stretch to Your knees. Bend Your ear down a minute, I want to tell You a secret. I think You're wonderful. And I really do trust You. When I grow up I want to be just like You. *(NR/HW)*

Blessed is the man [woman] who makes the Lord his [her] trust.

PSALM 40:4

For you have been my hope, O Sovereign Lord, my confidence since my youth. From birth I have relied on you; you brought me forth from my mother's womb. I will ever praise you . . . Since my youth, O God, you have taught me, and to this day I declare your marvelous deeds. Even when I am old and gray, do not forsake me, O God, till I declare your power to the next generation, your might to all who are to come.

PSALM 71:5–6, 17–18

I will say of the Lord, "He is my refuge and my fortress, my God, in whom I trust."

PSALM 91:2

The Living Example

Wisdom is the acquired ability to live life well.
David Swartz, *Dancing with Broken Bones*

To live life well is to learn to live in the present and leave our past in the Father's hands. Jesus did this when, to follow God's will, He left behind His glory, authority, and power.

We have little more to leave behind than sin, brokenness, and failure, yet regret has a way of binding us to our past. We will break free only when our purpose for moving into the present becomes the same as Christ's purpose for coming to us.

Jesus came here to do the work of the Father. This meant He had to become a servant, to lay aside His heavenly advantage, and to learn to stay in tune with the Father's will one moment at a time.

We are called to do the same—to lay aside our earthly disadvantage and to live moment by moment in complete dependence on the Father's will.

Breaking free from the past and learning to live wisely in the present makes life less complicated, but it does not necessarily mean that it will be more comfortable.

Jesus is our example here too. Life was far from easy for Him. He left the halls of heaven, which reverberated with endless praise and adoration, and landed cold, wet, and squirming on a pile of straw. The government immediately began killing babies, seeking to end His life almost before it began. He and His family became refugees.

He grew up submitting himself to the teaching and discipline of a man and woman He had created. His preparation for ministry was forty days and nights alone in the desert with no food or water.

He spent the last three years of His life on earth with friends who couldn't grasp who He was or comprehend why He had come. They rarely understood what He was saying or why He said it. He was a constant wanderer. His family once decided He was crazy and tried to take Him back home.

Crowds hounded Him, seeking to use His goodness for their own gain. Church leaders lay in wait to bait and discredit Him. Even His closest friends eventually deserted, denied, and betrayed Him.

The work He had come to do included taking insults, floggings, false accusations, and bearing the most gruesome death imaginable at the hands of pompous, self-righteous men. But He chose to do all of this "for the joy set before Him."

When we are unable to celebrate the present because it is so painful, frustrating, or filled with stress, we need to follow the example of our Lord. We need to reach forward and pull some of the "joy set before us" into our present situation.

As we leave the past behind and borrow liberally from our hope of glory, we find that we can live and rejoice in the present. For God is among us. He is not called "I Was" or "I Will Be," but "I AM." He is here. Now. With us. Whatever is going on in our lives, we can celebrate Him! (*EBP*)

Let us fix our eyes on Jesus, the author and perfecter of our faith, who for the joy set before him endured the cross, scorning its shame, and sat down at the right hand of the throne of God. Consider him who endured such opposition from sinful men, so that you will not grow weary and lose heart.

HEBREWS 12:2–3

Anyone who says he is a Christian should live as Christ did.

1 JOHN 2:6 TLB

A student is not above his teacher, nor a servant above his master. It is enough for the student to be like his teacher, and the servant like his master.

MATTHEW 10:24–25

I have come that they may have life, and have it to the full.

JOHN 10:10

PART 2

Standing Firm through the Storm

When the storm has swept by, the wicked are gone, but the righteous stand firm forever.

Proverbs 10:25

If Grace Has a Lap

*Many Christians seem to understand the
concept of being saved by grace, but they have
missed the concept of being sustained by grace.*

James D. Mallory Jr., *The Kink and I*

Almighty God,
   great and
   majestic,
I know that You encircle the
   needs of your children
with the broad embrace of
   eternal solution.
But Abba Father,
   do not leave me
   struggling and unstroked
   upon this earth!
If grace has a lap,
   find and hold me there till

all my cries and longings
   snuggle at last into the
Arms of Peace. *(EBP)*

All my longings lie open before you, O Lord; my sighing is not hidden from you . . . As the deer pants for streams of water, so my soul pants for you, O God. My soul thirsts for God, for the living God. When can I go and meet with God?

PSALM 38:9; 42:1–2

He tends his flock like a shepherd: He gathers the lambs in his arms and carries them close to his heart; he gently leads those that have young.

ISAIAH 40:11

Do not fear, for I am with you; do not be dismayed, for I am your God. I will strengthen you and help you; I will uphold you with my righteous right hand.

ISAIAH 41:10

My grace is sufficient for you, for my power is made perfect in weakness.

2 CORINTHIANS 12:9

Seeing Beneath and Beyond

You are looking only on the surface of things.
2 Corinthians 10:7

*L*ooking at the surface of life's present circumstances I can come to several conclusions, all of them factual, all of them miserable.

First, I'm being rained on. Again.

Second, I'm soaking wet and shivering in the winds of adversity. Again.

Third, if "wet is wonderful," then I'm more than wonderful because I'm completely and totally *drenched*.

Menacing storms like this one have been lined up on the horizon of my life like a fleet of planes in a relentless landing pattern.

And I can see absolutely no spiritual progress, no purpose, no good, no gain. From where I stand in the clouds and pouring rain, it's impossible to see what God is doing beneath the surface and beyond the moment.

It is possible, however, to *know* without seeing.

Because I know my heavenly Father. I know He's able to do anything, anywhere, in any weather condition, visibly or invisibly. And whatever He does will always turn out to be good, because *He* is good.

Without seeing, I know that these rains of adversity will soak deep into the soil of who I am and that through it all God will cause me to "take root below and bear fruit above" (2 Kings 19:30). And because of that Root, I will be "filled with the fruit of righteousness that comes through Jesus Christ—to the glory and praise of God" (Philippians 1:11).

God didn't say I should pretend to enjoy this tear-saturated and uncertain landscape. He did say that with eyes of faith I could see *beneath* it to His work within me, and *beyond* it to the joy set before me (Hebrews 12:2) . . . the joy set before *us*. He promised His eternal hope for tomorrow, and the grace and peace of His presence for today.

I'm not alone out in the rain. And neither are you. *(NR)*

We don't yet see things clearly. We're squinting in a fog, peering through a mist. But it won't be long before the weather clears and the sun shines bright! We'll see it all then, see it all as clearly as God sees us, knowing him directly just as he knows us!

1 CORINTHIANS 13:12 The Message

Now faith is being sure of what we hope for and certain of what we do not see . . .

Let us fix our eyes on Jesus, the author and perfecter of our faith, who for the joy set before him endured the cross, scoring its shame, and sat down at the right hand of the throne of God. Consider him who endured such opposition from sinful men, so that you will not grow weary and lose heart . . .

Endure hardship as discipline; God is treating you as sons. For what son is not disciplined by his father? If you are not discipline (and everyone undergoes discipline), then you are illegitimate children and not true sons. Moreover, we have all had human fathers who disciplined us and we respected them for it. How much more should we submit to the Father of our spirits and live! Our fathers disciplined us for a little while as they thought best; but God disciplines us for our good, that we may share in his holiness. No discipline seems pleasant at the time, but painful. Later on, however, it produces a harvest of righteousness and peace for those who have been trained by it.

HEBREWS 11:1; 12:2–3, 7–11

The Truth about Loss

In this world you will have trouble. But take heart! I have overcome the world.

Jesus, John 16:33

We don't like it, but we know that it's true: trouble is a natural part of living in this fallen world. The lessons come early and stay late.

As babies, we are wet and no one seems to notice. We cry and Mom doesn't rush to pick us up. Then one day we're expected to give up our warm bottle or breast for a cold hard cup. Our favorite blanket disappears in the wash. The stuffing comes out of our teddy bear. "No!" seems to be the answer for everything we want to touch or taste. Daddy keeps walking out the door, and Mommy spends too much time with that bawling little intruder. And these are the normal losses. There are worse.

As children, we find the excitement of going to school is tempered by having to leave the security of home. We learn that "F" stands for failure, not fun. We lose a friend to someone who's prettier or smarter. We are the last one picked for the team. We finally start liking the teacher, and then we're promoted to the next grade. And these are the normal losses. There are worse.

As teenagers, we find that our bodies and emotions are a foreign land with ever-changing boundaries. We feel okay about ourselves only if we lose our identity to fads and fashion. A broken romance shreds our heart. Our parents don't understand us. We've lost childhood and we can't find adulthood. And these are the normal losses. There are worse.

As adults, instead of celebrating the freedom we expected, we find ourselves tied to a job, a family, and a schedule. Babies cry and throw up. Kids argue and whine. Teens announce their superiority. Our grand dream for how life should be whimpers and slides sideways. People change, disappoint, fail, and leave us. Society is a mess. Gray hairs emerge. We lose our ability to lose weight. The children grow up and move out. Wrinkles and arthritis move in. We can't remember where we put our glasses. And these are the normal losses. There are worse.

We cope with these everyday losses fairly well. We adjust our attitude or change our perspective, method, or approach. Some losses we consciously grieve. Others we hardly notice because they occur so slowly. Occasionally we discover within life's process of loss and change the potential for growth, compassion, or a larger view. Sometimes we settle for simple survival. But we keep moving ahead with creative persistence. This is, after all, life. And these are life's normal losses. There are worse.

Internal losses are worse. These are the deprivations and abuses that seem to be a normal part of life, but are not. They rob us of love, trust, self-esteem, confidence, and a sense of worthiness and leave us feeling inadequate, inferior, unlovable. We bleed internally.

And what about life's land-mine losses? These are the explosions we never expected, didn't deserve, and couldn't prevent. They rip our world apart, leaving gaping holes where something, or someone, important used to be. They strike at our foundation and leave us lonely, lost, frightened, angry, insecure, and needy.

How do we deal with *these*, life's worst kind of losses?

If we're wise, we treat them with tenderness, patience, and God's help. We are hurting because we have serious wounds that need healing. And healing takes time. It also takes co-operation with God.

He whose hand formed us knows how to put us back together when life's losses have left us in pieces. Whether we are being pruned, tested, or have simply been caught in the rain that "falls on the just and unjust," He will bring us through. He is the great Healer. He is unequaled at creating something from nothing. He even knows how to bring life from death. So certainly we can trust Him with our pain, our loss, our brokenness, our very lives.

Perhaps too it will help to realize that we are more practiced in dealing with loss than we know. After all, we've made it this far. *(WLT)*

———————— ✌ ————————

"For I know the plans I have for you," declares the Lord, "plans to prosper you and not to harm you, plans to give you hope and a future."

JEREMIAH 29:11

Record my lament; list my tears on your scroll—are they not in your record?

PSALM 56:8

I have heard your prayer and seen your tears; I will heal you.

2 KINGS 20:5

"I am with you and will save you," declares the Lord . . . "I will restore you to health and heal your wounds."

JEREMIAH 30:11, 17

Dear Hurting One

My mouth would encourage you;
comfort from my lips would bring you relief.

Job 16:5

The measure of loss you are experiencing is
beyond my emotional comprehension.
Yet I ache with you and
long to lift your load,
even while knowing that you alone must carry
one grief at a time to
the God of all comfort.
How I pray that He will lead you daily
to the storehouse of His
grace, compassion, and healing.
And on that day when I need
help through grief's dark night,
I pray that God will grant me
the tender gift of you. *(WLT)*

Praise be to the God and Father of our Lord Jesus Christ, the Father of compassion and the God of all comfort, who comforts us in all our troubles, so that we can comfort those in any trouble with the comfort we ourselves have received from God. For just as the sufferings of Christ flow over into our lives, so also through Christ our comfort overflows.

2 CORINTHIANS 1:3–5

When the Wind Stops

God tempers the wind to the shorn lamb.
Laurence Sterne

My clock radio was trying to get my attention, pulling me out of another night of exhausted sleep, annoying me to consciousness with chatter and laughter. Eventually I realized I was hearing jokes about the weather from various parts of the country.

"It's so windy where we live," someone was saying, "that one day the wind stopped and everybody fell down!"

My mind awakened just in time to comprehend this scene, and God broke through to me with its graphic truth. From my prone position I saw a clear picture of my own weary situation.

The winds of trouble and stress had been blowing so long and unrelentingly in my life that I had learned to compensate—to lean into the wind just to stay erect. And when the blast of adversity finally stopped, I fell flat on my face.

There I lay, fatigued from battling my way forward against the gale forces, hurt from the fall, and no longer sure I could walk the narrow way, even if I could summon the energy to struggle to my feet. The old mandate to "pick yourself up, brush yourself off, and start all over again" had lost its appeal. I couldn't get up. So I found myself praying the most theologically correct prayer anyone in that position could ever pray. I said, "Help, Lord." That was all. Not even an amen.

For the first time in a long time, I began to rest in the knowledge that God knew where I was. He knew, and now I understood afresh that I couldn't stand in my own strength. While flat on my face, I had taken a big step toward finding God's sufficiency.

However, finding God's sufficiency and being able to appropriate it are two different matters. So I assigned myself a new task: "Stand in the strength of the Lord. Get up and walk! Grab hold of *His* strength!"

But God, who is rich in mercy, quickly pointed out that only He can make us stand. And He does not require us to grasp for His strength. That would be an equally ineffective form of "doing it myself." A weak hand holding onto a strong arm forms a weak bond. It is when strength takes hold of weakness that we can rest, knowing that "underneath are the everlasting arms."

The God of all comfort cares for His hurting, weary children. He waits to hear our cry, waits to lift us out of the pit and hold us close to His heart. When He has nourished and strengthened us, then He will teach us how to walk in the calm as well as in the wind. *(EBP)*

Before they call I will answer; while they are still speaking I will hear.

ISAIAH 65:24

This is what the Lord says: "I will extend peace to her like a river . . . As a mother comforts her child, so will I comfort you."

ISAIAH 66:12–13

I have made you and I will carry you; I will sustain you and I will rescue you . . . I am God, and there is none like me.

ISAIAH 46:4, 9

The God of all grace, who called you to his eternal glory in Christ, after you have suffered a little while, will himself restore you and make you strong, firm and steadfast. To him be the power for ever and ever. Amen.

1 PETER 5:10–11

Dear Grieving One

Loss and suffering, joyfully accepted for the kingdom of God, show the supremacy of God's worth more clearly in the world than all the worship and prayer.

John Piper

As I pray for you, I see God there with you—the Answer who doesn't always speak the answers, but just is. He is holding you tenderly in His arms and pressing you close to His great heartbeat of compassion, letting His tears mingle with yours. His sweet breath is gently ruffling your hair with wordless whispers of hope in the night.

Let Him hold you for as long as it takes. Thank Him for all the wonderful people He has brought into your life over the years, and let them hold you for as long as it takes. You might need to explain that you need them to listen and care, but not try to fix you or make the pain go away. They will be helped as they share your hurt, and so will you.

Cry as much and as often as you need or want to. Weeping is not weakness. Feeling as though you're "falling apart" is not an indication of a failing testimony. Doubts and questions don't insult or frighten God, so speak freely to Him. He wants your whole heart, even if it comes to Him in broken, jagged pieces.

There are no "timetables" on grief. There is no "right way" for everyone to grieve. But there are some things you can do to move through grief in healthy ways. Like taking care of yourself, asking for prayer, facing rather than avoiding the pain, perhaps joining a grief support group, constantly leaning on God, and thanking and praising Him as you inch forward. But they're not quick fixes.

There may be those who suggest that deep or prolonged grief—with its attendant doubts, questions, and often anger— indicates a lack of trust in God or a failure to rely on Him. They believe that stoic bravery or a "quick recovery" is a credit to God's reputation and yours. Perhaps they think that refusing to express painful feelings is a way to snuff them out. They don't understand. We are glad they haven't yet had reason to.

Lack of trust will, indeed, prolong the pain and isolate us from God's full comfort, but feelings of doubt, rage, or engulfing loneliness come even to those who fully trust God. It is a part of honest grief to express them before the Lord.

Knowing that your loved one is with God doesn't erase the agony that he or she is no longer with you on this earth. Knowing that Christ conquered death eternally doesn't nullify the pain of separation now. God created the process of grief as His path through the losses of this sin-riddled world.

The integrity of emotional and spiritual honesty requires us to walk that painful but hope-filled path.

Try writing letters to God and letters to your loved one. Often that helps. And expect to deal with a sense of confusion at times, even some inertia, for this is common. I can't tell you how many times I would go into a room and have no idea why I had gone there. I tend to do that on occasion anyway, but I did it again and again in the first weeks after Herb died. Deep grief is disorienting.

Be gentle with yourself. Don't rush into big changes. Eat right. Buy tons of soft Kleenex. Ask people for patience when you forget everything from their name to what you told them you would do. Wait in—not just on, but in—the Lord, and rest there. You don't have to do everything the way you used to do it. Concentrate on putting one foot in front of the other, living one moment at a time. After all, that's all we can ever live anyway.

Take to heart Jesus' words that "each day has enough trouble of its own," and consciously work at not taking on the whole load of frightening tomorrows. For Jesus is already living in tomorrow, working things out on your behalf. He is working at a leisurely pace. He's not nervous or concerned. He is preparing a table for you—with candlelight and roses and wonderful food—in the presence of your enemies. What a God, who sets up His dining room on the battlefront!

But even knowing these things, there will be times when you may fear that you won't survive the pain and waves of grief. But you will. Because God will not let go of you. He is faithful in this, too. Especially in this.

I celebrate with you those moments when you'll know and feel His precious presence, and I hold on in faith for you in those moments when you won't know or feel a thing but pain. Just remember, He is the same yesterday, today, and forever. And He loves you with a love that will not—indeed, cannot—let you go. There is healing in His wings. I know, for He has lifted me up on those healing wings. *(LH)*

Be merciful to me, O Lord, for I am in distress; my eyes grow weak with sorrow, my soul and my body with grief.
PSALM 31:9

Though he brings grief, he will show compassion, so great is his unfailing love. For he does not willingly bring affliction or grief to the children of men.
LAMENTATIONS 3:32–33

He will cover you with his feathers, and under his wings you will find refuge; his faithfulness will be your shield and rampart.
PSALM 91:4

136

Where Is Your Heart Today?

Now is your time of grief, but I will see you again and you will rejoice, and no one will take away your joy.

Jesus, John 16:22

Where is your heart today, My child?
　　Has it left you to follow,
　　　　weeping, after that precious
　　　　　　part of you that I have
　　　　　　　　taken home?
Your aching heart seeks that place
　　where your dear one
　　　　dances and sings beneath the
　　　　　　shadow of My wing.
One day, when your weeping slows,
　　and your heart wanders back to you
　　feeling bereft and stunned to silence by its
　　singularity,

it will make the wonderful discovery—
one that your head has long known—
that you, too, can live on
(though you haven't wanted to, I know).
And right there, alone in your house, you will learn to
dance and sing again
beneath the shadow of My wing.
Then your heart, too, will be home, My love. *(LH)*

On my bed I remember you; I think of you through the watches of the night. Because you are my help, I sing in the shadow of your wings. My soul clings to you; your right hand upholds me.

PSALM 63:6–8

Saying this often helped me. Substitute the name of your loved one who is with the Lord:

[Herb] is no longer on earth, therefore I hurt and grieve, yet I rejoice that [Herb] is with You, Lord. I am still on earth and though I hurt and grieve, yet I rejoice that You, Lord, are with me. So, in a deep, untouchable way, [Herb] and I are together still. Forever together in Christ.

Living the Questions

*If trust and love required full understanding,
children would never love their parents.*

Why do we want, and sometimes even demand, answers to the hard questions about life—those things that so wound and baffle us? What are we really asking when we badger God to tell us why He's allowing such painful things to happen?

"Why are children dying and killing one another?" "Why do we have disease and tragedy?" "Why is there betrayal and divorce?" "Why do we live with hate, cruelty, war, and destruction?" "Why are there earthquakes, floods, hurricanes?" "Why do even good people suffer?" "Why are You allowing me to suffer?" "Why are You allowing even this to be taken from me?"

Do our endless "why" questions suggest that we cannot, or will not, fully trust and love a God we cannot fully understand—a God who works in and through pain? Then surely we will never have the blessed peace of trusting and resting in Him on this earth. For even if He told us what we beg to know, our finite minds could not fully grasp our infinite God, or what He is accomplishing in us, and how, in the midst of this sin-riddled world.

Some people hold only a thin hope that God truly hears and answers prayers, or that His claims of being all-powerful and good are true. Some of these desperate people might be His own children who, day after day, live with their own tragedy and pain. Others listen to the evening news, trying to hide a growing suspicion that God is actually powerless against this world's evil. Their constant "why" questions demand that He prove himself.

Despite the fact that sin is here by human choice, people who doubt God in their pain refuse to fully embrace a God who claims a power over sin that He does not demonstrate by erasing evil and its consequences from our lives and world now. They fear serving a Jesus who seems to be ever standing before Pilate, whipped and beaten by wickedness, saying and doing nothing. Somehow His silent patience, then and now, is seen as impotence, or lack of love.

These dear ones miss the incredible power and love of our almighty Creator with a bowed head, wearing our crown of thorns.

This is a God who could and can lash back, eradicating sin and the sinner so steeped in it. Instantly. Yet He is a God who chose, and yet chooses, to bow His head and take our thorns. He will not always stand this way with His arms held out.

One day He will say, "Enough. I am coming to put an end to sin, and take those home with Me who would believe and gratefully live in a love they could not fully understand. I will gather those who came to Me as little children, who did not measure their Father's love by the circumstances in which they were loved."

As we live through the final death throes of wickedness in this world, we are watching and learning that sin is still deadly, and redemption still costly. Our patient, gracious, and compassionate God still waits and rescues from the midst.

At last we think to ask Him, not why He is yet allowing so much pain—clearly it is still here because sin and consequences are still here—but rather, why He stands with us in it, rescuing still?

And finally we hear God's gentle question. "Why are you so slow to ask Me to use these painful thorns in your life as part of My redemption plan? It's one of the things I do best, you know."

We don't need to understand any more than we have already learned from the foot of the cross, and the mouth of the empty tomb. We need comfort and hope more than we need answers. When we allow God to provide that, we can live life's painful questions until He fully reveals His secret wisdom in that final day. With His strength, and in His love, we can wait with patient joy even in the midst of tears. *(LH)*

We speak of God's secret wisdom, a wisdom that has been hidden and that God destined for our glory before time began. None of the rulers of this age understood it, for if they had, they would not have crucified the Lord of glory. However, as it is written: "No eye has seen, no ear has heard, no mind has conceived what God has prepared for those who love him"—but God has revealed it to us by his Spirit. The Spirit searches all things, even the deep things of God . . . "For who has known the mind of the Lord that he may instruct him?" But we have the mind of Christ.

1 CORINTHIANS 2:7–10, 16

We rejoice in the hope of the glory of God. Not only so, but we also rejoice in our sufferings, because we know that suffering produces perseverance; perseverance, character; and character, hope. And hope does not disappoint us, because God has poured out his love into our hearts by the Holy Spirit, whom he has given us.

ROMANS 5:2–5

Ministering Hope

> **The word which God has written on
> the brow of every man is Hope.**
> **Victor Hugo**

The first word to wither and drop from the vocabulary of the discouraged is *hope*. Even if Victor Hugo was right when he said that God has written *hope* on my forehead, I'm still in trouble. Reading my own forehead is about as easy as kissing my own elbow.

Then along come those who mirror the love of God, and I see Hope reflected in their eyes. And that Hope, I discover, is not a thing but a person—Jesus Christ. They bring Christ to me through a helping hand, a word of encouragement, a message of love, and a touch that heals. Through such ministrations, they stretch my soul to receive the great Hope.

Christ always ministered like this—stretching shrunken souls with acts of love and compassion before imparting the large truth of who He was. And still today He is not content to settle back in the easy chair of our affection. Everywhere

He looks, people are wounded and weary—giving up hope. He longs to go on ministering His Hope through us. (*WLT*)

May you always be doing those good, kind things which show that you are a child of God, for this will bring much praise and glory to the Lord.

PHILIPPIANS 1:11 TLB

Each one should use whatever gift he has received to serve others, faithfully administering God's grace in its various forms. If anyone speaks, he should do it as one speaking the very words of God. If anyone serves, he should do it with the strength God provides, so that in all things God may be praised through Jesus Christ.

1 PETER 4:10–11

We have this hope as an anchor for the soul, firm and secure.

HEBREWS 6:19

Running from God

❧

Be sure of this—that I am with you
always, even to the end of the world.
Jesus, Matthew 28:20 TLB

So, you're running away from God.
    Angry. Rebellious. Full of doubts.
Fearing the offense of disagreeing with Deity—
    fearing to question a God beyond question.
Is it possible God is more offended when we:
    imagine we can hide from omnipresence?
Think His ear may be too fragile
    for our pain?
Pretend He cannot hear our
    unvoiced anger?
Deny our doubt can find its
    answer within Him?
Decide that mercy cannot meet us
    where we are?
Refuse the second chance He's
    offering right now? *(LH)*

Oh, how kind our Lord was, for he showed me how to trust him and become full of the love of Christ Jesus. How true it is, and how I long that everyone should know it, that Christ Jesus came into the world to save sinners—and I was the greatest of them all. But God had mercy on me so that Christ Jesus could use me as an example to show everyone how patient he is with even the worst sinners, so that others will realize that they, too, can have everlasting life. Glory and honor to God forever and ever. He is the King of the ages, the unseen one who never dies; he alone is God, and full of wisdom. Amen.

PAUL, 1 TIMOTHY 1:14–17 TLB

Not What You Wanted

"My thoughts are not your thoughts, neither are your ways my ways," declares the Lord. "As the heavens are higher than the earth, so are my ways higher than your ways and my thoughts than your thoughts."

Isaiah 55:8–9

Jesus' bewildered disciples watched in fear and disbelief as this Master they had followed, loved, and trusted for three years willingly walked into a situation where He was lied about, tortured, and hammered onto a cross to die. It was horrifying. Mind-boggling. It simply couldn't be right. Surely there must be some mistake. He had said He was God, yet there He hung, dying in agony!

This was not at all what they were expecting from Him.

This was not at all what they wanted.

This was not at all what they hoped for.

But it was what they needed. Their hope for eternal life depended upon it.

Is there something in your life right now that is not what you were expecting from God?

Not what you wanted, or hoped for at all?

Do you think God can produce eternal good through it anyway—no matter how awful it is?

He has a very good track record with that sort of thing, you know. *(LH)*

Jesus replied, "The hour has come for the Son of Man to be glorified. I tell you the truth, unless a kernel of wheat falls to the ground and dies, it remains only a single seed. But if it dies, it produces many seeds. The man who loves his life will lose it, while the man who hates his life in this world will keep it for eternal life. Whoever serves me must follow me; and where I am, my servant also will be. My Father will honor the one who serves me.

"Now my heart is troubled, and what shall I say? 'Father, save me from this hour'? No, it was for this very reason I came to this hour. Father, glorify your name!"

Then a voice came from heaven, "I have glorified it, and will glorify it again."

JOHN 12:23–28

Faith's Last Leap

*I have fought the good fight, I have
finished the race, I have kept the faith.*
2 Timothy 4:7

The day after my mother died, I was leafing through her
favorite daily devotional guide when I came across a loose
page torn and saved from some other book.

Carefully removing it, I read of a young boy's experience
writing and mailing his very first letter. Painstakingly he
had printed, "Dear Grandpa," and then spelled out what he
wanted for his birthday. At last, satisfied with the wording of
his request, he put his letter in an envelope and walked with
his mother to the mailbox. She lifted him up and said, "Let
it go." The boy hesitated. Would Grandpa really receive the
letter if he dropped it into the big, dark box? But he did let go,
and when the young boy received his grandfather's present he
also received his first lesson in trust.

As I sat there I recalled my dear mother's *last* lesson in
trust. I had watched her struggle between hanging on to this

life and letting go of it—struggle against leaving this earth and the people she loved so dearly—repeatedly fighting her way back from the banks of the River Jordan for one more kiss, one more smile, one more touch, just one more "I love you."

It must take a lot of faith to let go when God says it is time to cross the dark chasm that separates the earthly life we know from the unknown glories beyond. It is faith's last great effort. But when we do, how swiftly faith must become sight and darkness become eternal light.

Right now, as I speculate as to the glories of heaven and the beauty of the Savior who gave himself as a ransom for us, I can see my mother looking into His eyes. And I know her, she is roaming through gardens of delight arm in arm with Him, exclaiming over fragrances she never dreamed existed and admiring colors that He didn't put in our rainbow. (*WLT*)

Praise be to the God and Father of our Lord Jesus Christ! In his great mercy he has given us new birth into a living hope through the resurrection of Jesus Christ from the dead, and into an inheritance that can never perish, spoil or fade—kept in heaven for you, who through faith are shielded by God's power until the coming of the salvation that is ready to be revealed in the last time. In this you greatly rejoice, though now for a little while you may have

had to suffer grief in all kinds of trials. These have come so that your faith—of greater worth than gold, which perishes even though refined by fire—may be proved genuine and may result in praise, glory and honor when Jesus Christ is revealed.

1 PETER 1:3–7

Where You Find Me

If your heart is broken, you'll find God right there; if you're kicked in the gut, he'll help you catch your breath.

Psalm 34:18 The Message

Did you know, My child, that
where you find Me
determines what you know of Me?
I am vast, yet intimate and present.
When you find Me in your busy days,
you discover the Lord of daily things.
In chaos and crisis,
I come as peace and control.
In creation's abundance,
delight in My beauty and order.
In sin and failure,
revel in My grace and power to save.
In loss and heartache,
rest in My compassion and love.

When you go to the depths,
you find Me deeper still.
There is always more of Me.
I wait to be discovered. *(LH)*

Can you fathom the mysteries of God? Can you probe the limits of the Almighty?

Job 11:7

We know about these things because God has sent his Spirit to tell us, and his Spirit searches out and shows us all of God's deepest secrets. No one can really know what anyone else is thinking, or what he is really like, except that person himself. And no one can know God's thoughts except God's own Spirit. And God has actually given us his Spirit (not the world's spirit) to tell us about the wonderful free gifts of grace and blessing that God has given us.

1 Corinthians 2:10–12 TLB

Caught Off Balance

*For I am the Lord, your God, who
takes hold of your right hand and says
to you, Do not fear; I will help you.*

Isaiah 41:13

Sudden loss, besides leaving us hurt and bewildered, can leave us listing seriously to one side. This state of imbalance is surprising, if not downright frightening. We had no idea we were leaning so heavily on a person, job, or ability until it was yanked away without warning.

When a loved one who partially defines who we are (or who we are *not*) is taken away by death, distance, divorce, or disagreement, our grief is intensified by the loss of this part of ourselves. Maybe we had depended on the person to express emotion for us or to think or decide for us. Perhaps the person was our sense of humor, our planner, our conscience, our practical side, our memory, or even our proof of worth. In one way or another, that person was our *balance*. And now we are *off* balance.

It is not just the loss of a person that can throw us off balance. Sometimes the loss of a job, ability, ideal, attribute, or goal carries with it a large chunk of our self-esteem, identity, or purpose, leaving us feeling lopsided and ready to topple over. When this happens, it may be time to confess that our sense of well-being was improperly anchored. We may also discover that our vision needs to expand—that who we are is more than what we do or how we look, and that the sum of our worth is far more than any loss.

God's secure love and His sure promise to care for us are the perfect ballast; they provide stability without adding weight to our load. When our lives are filled with Jesus Christ and the security, worth, and identity He provides, the losses we experience cannot destabilize us.

We may still toss and turn in stormy weather, but we'll never run aground or be shipwrecked. *(WLT)*

Find rest, O my soul, in God alone; my hope comes from him. He alone is my rock and my salvation; he is my fortress, I will not be shaken. My salvation and my honor depend on God; he is my mighty rock, my refuge. Trust in him at all times, O people; pour out your hearts to him, for God is our refuge.

PSALM 62:5–8

I waited patiently for the Lord; he turned to me and heard my cry. He lifted me out of the slimy pit, out of the mud and mire; he set my feet on a rock and gave me a firm place to stand. He put a new song in my mouth, a hymn of praise to our God. Many will see and fear and put their trust in the Lord. Blessed is the man who makes the Lord his trust, who does not look to the proud, to those who turn aside to false gods.

PSALM 40:1–4

Stretching without Breaking

In him all things hold together.
Colossians 1:17

Certain days are designed for the sole purpose of expanding our coping ability. I did not learn this directly from Scripture. I learned it directly from life.

After one particular morning in which my coping ability was stretched, yanked, and nearly disjointed, I sat down and poured out my woes in a letter to a friend. (I chose this friend because she's single and her frustrations don't include kid stuff, so I get a lot of sympathy from her!)

I wrote:

> I was exhausted last night and had a nasty headache
> coming on, so Herb told me not to get up and fix
> breakfast . . . said I was to sleep in. The only way
> I could have accomplished that was to have been

unconscious—which, as I see it now, would have been nice.

With only three children in the house you'd think there would be a mathematical limitation to the possible combinations of fighting pairs, but this morning they exceeded the known possibilities. And when I stepped in to prevent further damage, I only increased the combinations by adding myself to the list!

Everybody was totally innocent, yet everybody was on the attack. Herb had an early flight to Los Angeles, but he told Jeff he'd drive him to school if he was ready by 7 a.m. Jeff wasn't ready (fighting takes time) so Herb had to leave to catch his plane.

He left me with one raging and frantic kid and two possible vehicles with which to transport him (assuming I could hold my throbbing head together and get dressed in time). One vehicle had a flat tire, which no one could explain, and the other had windshield wipers that work only in the sunshine— and of course it was raining.

But I had another idea for a way to get him there. I dressed quickly as frantic announcements of the time came at fifteen-second intervals.

The phone rang. It was Herb. He had barely made it to the airport and his plane was about to leave, but he was wondering how things were going!

When I told him, he came up with the same solution I had just hit upon . . . use the car our friend had left with us.

When I finally got that car warmed up I discovered that the knob labeled "wipers" wouldn't budge the wipers no matter which way I moved it! Jeff ran off in the downpour in an absolute frenzy. (What do they do to kids who are late that triggers such panic?!)

The condition of the house after the kids whirled through it matches the condition of my head. As I write this, ants are marching across the counter feasting on the rich ravages of a kitchen where three kids simply fixed cereal! There goes the phone again.

I recognized the voice at the other end right away because it said, "Mom?" in this I've-got-a-problem-and-it's-all-your-fault-so-you'd-better-help-me-out tone of voice.

"What, Matthew?" I asked in a patient now-I've-got-the-problem-but-what-else-is-new tone of voice.

"You knew I needed valentines today because we're having our party and you didn't get them for me."

"How could I know, Matt? You never told me." I couldn't resist using logic, even on a morning like this.

"Well I have to have them," he said flatly.

So now I have to go out in the rain without a decent car and find cutesy little paper hearts for my son to give to his classmates who probably don't care anyway.

When I get back home—if I ever do—I have to take a shower (though maybe I can skip that after running around in the rain), and then I have to get ready to go speak to thirty pastors on the ministry of counseling. I'll tell you who needs the ministry of counseling about now, old friend!

When we reach the end of our ability to cope, when we are at the absolute end of our rope, it is in Christ that we need to place our hope. For in Him—and only in Him—all things hold together. He offers peace, rest, and the renewal of our minds, hearts, and coping ability. *(EBP)*

In Christ all the fullness of the Deity lives in bodily form, and you have been given fullness in Christ, who is the head over every power and authority . . . Therefore, as God's chosen people, holy and dearly loved, clothe yourselves with compassion, kindness, humility, gentleness and patience. Bear with each other and forgive whatever grievances you may have against one another. Forgive as the

Lord forgave you. And over all these virtues put on love,
which binds them all together in perfect unity.

COLOSSIANS 2:9–10; 3:12–14

Daily Sprinkles

Consider it pure joy, my brothers, whenever you face
trials of many kinds, because you know that the
testing of your faith develops perseverance.

James 1:2–3

I want to grow, Lord.
It's all right with me
if You send some trial my way
so I'll learn to lean on Your strength.
Don't spare me by making it small—
send a big biblical blast of
holy refining fire.
Don't let my bickering children,
this tension headache,
the incessantly ringing telephone,
these broken dishes,
this draining tiredness,
the heat and smog,
or these boring repetitive tasks

distract me—
so that when a trial comes
I miss it.
It would be such a shame
if I overlooked my chance
to grow closer to You! (NR)

You let the distress bring you to God, not drive you from him. The result was all gain, no loss. Distress that drives us to God does that. It turns us around. It gets us back in the way of salvation. We never regret that kind of pain. But those who let distress drive them away from God are full of regrets, end up on a deathbed of regrets. And now, isn't it wonderful all the ways in which this distress has goaded you closer to God? You're more alive, more concerned, more sensitive, more reverent, more human, more passionate, more responsible. Looked at from any angle, you've come out of this with purity of heart.

2 CORINTHIANS 7:9–11 *The Message*

The Present

**Therefore God again set a
certain day, calling it Today.**
Hebrews 4:7

You can only live one day at a time, they say. And they are right!

Not one of us has more than the present moment to live—and do—and be. Yet how often we forfeit today to discontent, depression, and frustration over what is past or what might lie ahead.

Stephanie Edwards, a familiar redheaded television personality here on the West Coast, is a believer who occasionally struggles with depression. She offers insight to people who give away the "now moments"—the only sure gift that time offers. "People who are depressed," she says, "feel bad about the past, dread the future, and discount the present."

For many, depression is the result of a stressful life, unresolved conflicts, or losses. For some it is the manifestation of a physical problem such as a chemical imbalance or illness. But

164

whatever its cause, and even though it can sometimes be the result of sin or even lead to sin, in its purest form depression is a state, not a sin. And it is never pleasant.

Yet even in the midst of depression, we can ask the Lord to help us find a way to change what we need to change—one small step at a time—and to accept the rest. If we ask our Savior to make us truly content in "whatever state we find ourselves," something begins to change in us and gradually we are able to appreciate God's gift of the present moment.

Stephanie Edwards has found a way to do this. "If we can learn to live life in fifteen minute chunks," she explains, "it forces us to pray constantly, enables us to give worth to this moment's activity, and causes us to see the Lord present—right here, right now."

Learning to live in fifteen-minute chunks may be easier for Stephanie than for the rest of us, since she's used to having television commercials! But if we try her wisdom, it may help us live a life of eternal significance whatever each day brings to us. (EBP)

───────────── ✣ ─────────────

The Lord is near. Do not be anxious about anything, but in everything, by prayer and petition, with thanksgiving, present your requests to God. And the peace of God,

*which transcends all understanding, will guard your
hearts and your minds in Christ Jesus.*

PHILIPPIANS 4:5–7

*I have learned to be content whatever the circumstances. I
know what it is to be in need, and I know what it is to have
plenty. I have learned the secret of being content in any
and every situation, whether well fed or hungry, whether
living in plenty or in want. I can do everything through
him who gives me strength.*

PHILIPPIANS 4:11–13

Letter to a Friend

**It's our job to introduce our circumstances
and feelings to God's resurrection truth.**

*M*y Dear Friend,

I had such a wonderful time with you the other afternoon, but my heart has been so heavy with your situation and concerns since we talked. I keep praying that God will keep you balanced. You are dealing with so much stress from so many different areas!

It's ironic that I'm in the midst of writing a book about growing through life's storms. When I think of how you're struggling, I am cautioned not to toss out a simplistic challenge to people I've never even met to "trust and *grow* through it all!" (I already felt cautious, but even more so now!)

I know it's not easy to trust and look for growth when nothing makes sense—when you're about to lose everything—when there's no peace anywhere—when you feel as if you're the only one in the boat who's rowing. It's all too easy to feel abandoned by an all-powerful, limitless Lord who doesn't appear to be using His power and riches to help when you're clearly going down for the count!

I can't give you (or anyone else) platitudes or easy answers. Because there *are no* easy answers. But I can hold on in faith for you . . . faith in a God of love who won't let us go no matter how bad it looks or feels . . . faith in the work He's doing in you and through you, His beloved child, my dear sister.

And if it does get worse—if God allows you to lose even more that is precious to you—you can be certain that I won't understand or like it any better than you do. I'll probably ask God if He's *sure* this is necessary. I'll probably tell Him you didn't *need* that. I might even get into the subject of what's "fair" and "not fair," like my kids used to do. Because I know that you're doing everything you can possibly do!

But then I'll have to wipe my eyes and go on trusting Him with you. And I'll need to begin praising Him for that hard-to-imagine good that He's *covenanted* to work out for you. Because while I don't want to see you *hurting*, I know that He won't allow you to be truly *harmed*—even when it hurts and feels like the bottom has dropped out.

May I share one thing with you? When I was carrying you in my heart (everywhere I went the other morning!), I happened to be reading Ray Stedman's book *God's Loving Word*. He was discussing John 19:41–42, which tells us about Joseph of Arimathea and Nicodemus laying Jesus' body in a new tomb in a garden near the place where He was crucified.

Ray writes:

> There, in that beautiful garden, just a few yards
> from the site of Jesus' agony, was this tomb. The
> cross represented failure and despair.
>
> Certainly, that was the mood of all those who
> had followed Jesus throughout His earthly ministry,
> only to see all their hopes nailed to a Roman cross.
>
> But, though Jesus' friends and followers didn't
> know it then, the place of resurrection was just a few
> yards from the place of despair and hopelessness.
> And so it is with you and me.
>
> Perhaps you are feeling a complete bankruptcy of
> spirit as you read these words. Perhaps you are in a
> situation which leaves you feeling hopeless. Perhaps,
> you have been "crucified," unjustly treated by the
> world around you. Your spirit may be broken, and
> you see no future ahead of you.
>
> Let me assure you of this: There is a resurrection
> in your future. You can't see it now, but it is not far
> away. The empty tomb is near the cross. When you
> stand close to the cross of Jesus, when you choose to
> follow the will of God wherever it leads, the Day of
> Resurrection is just around the corner!

I wait with you, my precious friend. And I hurt and wonder with you. But I also know (as I'm sure some part of you
does too) that God has a great "gettin' up mornin'" around

the corner for you and your precious family. That corner just won't come soon enough for either one of us!

I love you, I believe in you, and I'll ride this out with you. Susan *(NR)*

It is right for me to feel this way about . . . you, since I have you in my heart.

Philippians 1:7

May our Lord Jesus Christ himself and God our Father, who loved us and by his grace gave us eternal encouragement and good hope, encourage your hearts and strengthen you in every good deed and word . . . The Lord is faithful, and he will strengthen and protect you from the evil one . . . May the Lord direct your hearts into God's love and Christ's perseverance.

2 Thessalonians 2:16–17; 3:3, 5

In Deep Shadow

We look for light, but all is darkness; for brightness, but we walk in deep shadows.

Isaiah 59:9

Dear child of God,
When clouds descend,
when depression wraps its
heavy cloak about your soul,
when God seems distant and
you, so alone—
stretch out a finger of faith,
for you may be closer than you've
ever been . . .
He may be hiding you in the
shadow of His wing.
Beneath God's wing
deep shadow blocks our sight
and bids us hear our
darkest feelings whisper

their pain, loss, and unmet needs
into the sufficiency of God's love. *(WLT)*

He who dwells in the shelter of the Most High will rest in the shadow of the Almighty. I will say of the Lord, "He is my refuge and my fortress, my God, in whom I trust." Surely he will save you from the fowler's snare and from the deadly pestilence. He will cover you with his feathers, and under his wings you will find refuge; his faithfulness will be your shield and rampart. You will not fear the terror of night, nor the arrow that flies by day, nor the pestilence that stalks in the darkness, nor the plague that destroys at midday . . .

"Because he loves me," says the Lord, "I will rescue him; I will protect him, for he acknowledges my name. He will call upon me, and I will answer him; I will be with him in trouble, I will deliver him and honor him. With long life will I satisfy him and show him my salvation."

PSALM 91:1–6, 14–16

Oh, God, Why?

*Why have you made me your target? . . . Why do you
hide your face? . . . Why should I struggle in vain? . . .
Why does the Almighty not set times for judgment?
. . . Why then did you bring me out of the womb?*

Job 7:20; 13:24; 9:29; 24:1; 10:18

I have often heard it said that people facing loss and
pain should never ask why. At best, claim the critics, such
questioning is counterproductive. At worst, it's a sign we're
not trusting God.

Why do these people say such things? Perhaps they don't
understand the question. To cry out "Oh God, *why?*" is the
natural response of a soul facing the terrible consequences of
living in a sin-filled world. The knowledge that such agony
was never part of God's plan for us, and thus can never seem
"right," bursts from our spirit in the form of a cry that inevitably begins with *why*.

"Why am I alone now?"

"Why is my world falling apart?"

"Why have I been betrayed?"

"Why does God seem so far away when I need Him most?"

"Why did this innocent child have to suffer and die?"

"Why is life so full of pain?"

We cling to the knowledge that God has already won the victory over death. But physical—and often painful—death is still our passageway to receive the prize of eternal life and freedom from sin's ravage.

How true that God plants seeds of hope within every thorny situation. Hope, however, does not remove life's thorns and thistles. Even though we know that loss and separation cannot harm us eternally, the hurt on this earth can at times be almost unbearable.

No one understands this better than Jesus. After hanging on a cross for three hours in utter darkness, suspended by spikes through his hands and feet while the accumulated sins of humankind were heaped upon His bleeding back, our Lord cried out through parched and swollen lips, "My God, my God, *why* have you forsaken me?"

This couldn't have been a real question from One who had all wisdom and knowledge. He *knew* why. Together, He and the Father had built this terrifying moment of redemption into the foundation of the world! Yet His suffering, lonely spirit could not keep from crying out, "Why God? *Why*? How can I bear this all alone?"

Through the tears of a loving Savior who knows the depths of what we suffer in ways we can never fathom, God hears our wrenching cries of "Oh God, *why?*"

His answers are being held tenderly in a nailed-pierced hand. (*WLT*)

What, then, shall we say in response to this? If God is for us, who can be against us? He who did not spare his own Son, but gave him up for us all—how will he not also, along with him, graciously give us all things?

ROMANS 8:31–32

I am convinced that neither death nor life, neither angels nor demons, neither the present nor the future, nor any powers, neither height nor depth, nor anything else in all creation, will be able to separate us from the love of God that is in Christ Jesus our Lord.

ROMANS 8:38–39

No Simple Losses

Sometimes it takes a long, long time before we can glean enrichment from the deprivation and suffering which has baffled and overwhelmed us.

Mildred Tengbom

Sure I've suffered a loss," you say to yourself, "and I'll admit it's been tough. But I should be able to get through this thing by now!" And you push at yourself, impatient with your progress—or seeming lack of it.

The trouble is while you weren't looking, this *thing* you were dealing with became these *things*. Loss is never simple.

Our newly married daughter discovered this unfortunate truth when, for reasons unknown, the cartilage in her hip degenerated. Through four surgeries and two terrible years, she didn't walk a step. Simply put, Cathy lost her mobility. But that's not all she lost. Loss has a way of hemorrhaging. It bleeds into so many areas of what we do and who we are.

At a time when Cathy was just establishing her independence, she lost it. She lost her freedom (even driving a car was impossible), her hope for the future (they were not sure she would ever walk again), and thus she also lost her confidence and sense of control over her own life. She was unable to keep her job, manage her home, carry on a normal married life, or enjoy her usual pursuits. She and her new husband lost control of their finances as medical bills and worries mounted. Rather than sharing joys and hopes, she and her husband, Wes, shared struggles, fears, and disappointments.

She was no longer certain who she was. It affected all of her relationships, plans, and activities. Constant pain, interruptions for surgeries, and ongoing uncertainty left her unable to continue her college education or plan for a family. She was at the mercy of new medical techniques.

She would recover from a pioneering surgical procedure by top specialists only to be worse off than before. After one operation, she spent six weeks at our house flat on her back in a hospital bed attached to a machine that kept her leg slowly moving. There were bedpans, sponge baths, and visiting hours in our family room. Her emotional stamina deteriorated along with her physical strength. The losses were complicated and demanding. The doctors didn't know what else to do for her.

Then her doctor heard of a new technique. It had never been used in a case exactly like hers, but it might work. She was scheduled for one more surgery. When the day came, I drove for hours through rush hour traffic after leaving the cemetery where I had just watched my mother's casket being lowered into the ground. It was a day I could never have imagined. Mom was gone, and this was to be my daughter's last hope for walking.

At three o'clock in the morning, Cathy was wheeled back into her room. The weary surgeon was optimistic. It had gone well.

Months later, and for the second time in my life, I had the joy of watching my daughter take her first struggling steps. She would still need crutches, and then a cane, for a long time. But there was hope.

Time has passed. There are still limitations, but Cathy is walking again. We are all so thankful. The passage of time, however, doesn't dim the fact that those were very difficult years—made even more difficult because during that same period Wes lost three jobs due to company shutdowns, his father was killed in an auto accident, and his mother suffered two heart attacks. Loss gangs up on us sometimes.

It takes all the distance and perspective that time can afford to find the gleanings of good amid such suffering, but they are there. We are all more patient now with the complexity of loss; we understand that adjusting and healing have their own schedule.

I have watched Cathy discover who she really is and find joy wherever it is available. Things that used to upset her no longer have the same disruptive power. She knows now what's really important. She and her precious husband have grown close through this time that tried its best to tear them apart. They are both stronger in character and coping abilities. They know that life and love are our most treasured gifts.

Today I asked Cathy what she would tell you—what she has learned through all of this. She laughed and said, "How long is this book? My whole *attitude* is different. And I'm still learning.

"You know that I've always been strong—determined." (Yes, I know!) "But now I understand that willpower alone can't always get you what you want. I had to learn to trust. And now I find that I have such compassion for people who are hurting or in trouble. I'm not quick to blame them for their condition—I just want to find a way to help.

"And I'm so thankful for the support of my family and friends. I have hope today because people cared and helped me get back on my feet!

"For a long time I was controlled by what I no longer had. Now I am able to focus on what I do have and be thankful. Now I treasure every moment—every experience and person. The other day I caught myself treasuring my husband *when he was in a bad mood!*"

And what would Cathy tell you as you struggle with your loss? What would *I* say to you? Be patient with yourself. Be kind to your hurts and needs. They may reach farther than you realize. Loss, after all, is not simple. *(WLT)*

Deep calls to deep in the roar of your waterfalls; all your waves and breakers have swept over me. By day the Lord directs his love, at night his song is with me—a prayer to the God of my life. I say to God my Rock, "Why have you forgotten me? Why must I go about mourning, oppressed by the enemy?" My bones suffer mortal agony as my foes taunt me, saying to me all day long, "Where is your God?" Why are you downcast, O my soul? Why so disturbed within me? Put your hope in God, for I will yet praise him, my Savior and my God.

PSALM 42:7–11

Thorns Will Increase

*Do not be afraid of what you are about
to suffer . . . Be faithful, even to the point
of death, and I will give you the crown of life.*

Revelation 2:10

Oh Christian,
kneel at Christ's feet as
evil ascends to power,
as arrogant men mock and lie and maim,
fists thrust into the face of the Almighty.
Do not be afraid.
Just stay at His nail-scarred feet and
praise Him as troubles mount,
as nation rises against nation and
our world seems to spiral out of control.
Wait patiently and pray,
for all that lifts itself up will
fall at the feet of this One you worship.

For He is Lord,
and every stiffened knee will one day
bow beside you. *(LH)*

You will hear of wars and rumors of wars, but see to it
that you are not alarmed. Such things must happen, but
the end is still to come. Nation will rise against nation,
and kingdom against kingdom. There will be famines and
earthquakes in various places. All these are the beginning of birth pains. Then you will be handed over to be
persecuted and put to death, and you will be hated by
all nations because of me. At that time many will turn
away from the faith and will betray and hate each other,
and many false prophets will appear and deceive many
people. Because of the increase of wickedness, the love of
most will grow cold, but he who stands firm to the end
will be saved.

JESUS, MATTHEW 24:6–13

*"As surely as I live," says the Lord, "every knee will bow
before me; every tongue will confess to God." So then,
each of us will give an account of himself to God.*

ROMANS 14:11–12

The Success of Failure

We all stumble in many ways.
James 3:2

*S*ome of life's clouds stay high above us and merely threaten. Some sprinkle or mist, and some pour torrents. Others seem to move right down to where we live, settle over us, and dim our view of who we are and what we can do.

One such cloud is the leaden fog bank of personal failure. It covers our souls like a damp blanket, depressing us and obscuring our judgment. Soon we are in danger of believing not simply that we have failed but that we are a *failure*. What a difference between the two!

To have *failed* is to have lived, tried, and been proven to be imperfect like everyone else. To have failed is to own more wisdom, understanding, and experience than do those who sit on life's sidelines playing it safe. To have failed is to claim a clearer knowledge of what not to do the next time. And to have failed is to have an opportunity to extend to ourselves the grace that God so freely extends to us.

We become a *failure* when we allow mistakes to take away our ability to learn, give, grow, and try again. We become a failure if we allow our transgressions to activate an internal voice of eternal self-blame and shame. We become a failure if we let the "shoulds" and the "if onlys" suck us into their mire. And we are a failure when we become content with failing.

The mire caused by our blunders, errors, and failings can become the quicksand that traps us in regret, or it can become the material we use to make building blocks of righteousness. God waits to give us another chance. His grace is well spent on fresh starts.

Cast your cares on the Lord and he will sustain you; he will never let the righteous fall.

PSALM 55:22

If the Lord delights in a man's way, he makes his steps firm; though he stumble, he will not fall, for the Lord upholds him with his hand.

PSALM 37:23–24

The Lord upholds all those who fall and lifts up all who are bowed down.

PSALM 145:14

To him who is able to keep you from falling and to present you before his glorious presence without fault and with great joy—to the only God our Savior be glory, majesty, power and authority, through Jesus Christ our Lord, before all ages, now forevermore! Amen.

JUDE 24–25

The Unspeakable

*Compassion invites the honesty that voices
the unspeakable and brings healing.*

I found my little friend hiding in a corner of the living room, kicking at the bottom of an easy chair and biting his lower lip. Clearly he had sought this lonely spot to deal with distress heavier than a three-year-old boy knew how to carry.

Kneeling beside him, I touched his shoulder. "What's the matter, Stevie?" I asked. "You seem so sad."

He turned toward the chair, covering his face with his hands, and I thought that this little one who laughed and hugged so easily was going to shut me out from his hurt. But then, with large, wet eyes, he turned and looked at me. "I'm mad with Mommy," he whispered, almost inaudibly.

"You're angry with your mommy?"

"Yes. She keeps going away. She always goes away to the hospital to be with sister 'cause Katy's sick. But I don't *want* her to." He drew in a deep shaky breath. "It's not good," he concluded. "It's not good for Mommy!"

"No," I agreed gently, "and it's not good for Stevie either, is it?"

"No, not good for Stevie either," he admitted, and then he wept without restraint.

I gathered him into my arms, rocked him, and kissed him, and whispered that I knew he felt so sad. I told him how special he was and how much his mommy missed him when she had to be away to help his baby sister get over her bad sickness.

It was then, as we snuggled together, that I found myself remembering the time, months earlier, when I had felt this way.

My precious friend had been sick with cancer, and I had been sick with a malignant sorrow at the thought of losing her. Wasn't she God's faithful, loving, and fruitful servant? Didn't the world need her? And, oh, didn't *I* need her?

So I, like Stevie, had withdrawn to a lonely spot, biting my lip for control, trying to hide my sadness, and trying to hide from God, for I was angry with my Lord. He had the power to prevent it—but hadn't.

He found me, though, and then urged me—helped me—to cry out my rage, frustration, and indignation. At His gentle yet insistent probing, prayers too wounded to dress themselves in acceptable, respectable phrases whispered, "Unfair! Unfair!" And finally even the unspeakable was spoken—"Yes, I am angry with You!" I wept then, without restraint, feeling that He should strike me down.

As I cradled Stevie in my arms, I remembered that day and, with renewed awe, realized again that God is our Father of intimate, loving compassion. And such compassion never reacts; it responds . . . invites . . . enfolds . . . no matter what we're feeling or trying to hide.

It's all right—
    questions, pain, and
    stabbing anger
    can be poured out to
the Infinite One and
    He will not be damaged.
Our wounded ragings will be
    lost in Him and
      we
        will
          be
            found.
For we beat on His chest
    from within
    the circle of His arms. *(WLT)*

Even now my witness is in heaven; my advocate is on high. My intercessor is my friend as my eyes pour out tears to God; on behalf of a man he pleads with God as a man pleads for his friend.

JOB 16:19–21

Therefore I will not keep silent; I will speak out in the anguish of my spirit, I will complain in the bitterness of my soul.

JOB 7:11

I cry aloud to the Lord; I lift up my voice to the Lord for mercy. I pour out my complaint before him; before him I tell my trouble.

PSALM 142:1–2

Pain

*He has seen but half the universe who
never has been shewn the house of Pain.*

Ralph Waldo Emerson

My life is
Your song, dear Lord,
and if you choose to
write that song,
in part,
in minor key,
give voice to sing despite
the taste of tears.
With hands hard-clasped
in pain,
and head bowed low
in trust,
I know you hear such
minor songs
as major praise. *(WLT)*

My eyes are ever on the Lord, for only he will release my feet from the snare. Turn to me and be gracious to me, for I am lonely and afflicted. The troubles of my heart have multiplied; free me from my anguish.

PSALM 25:15–17

Be merciful to me, O Lord, for I am in distress; my eyes grow weak with sorrow, my soul and my body with grief . . . But I trust in you, O Lord; I say, "You are my God." My times are in your hands.

PSALM 31:9, 14–15

The Lord is my strength and my shield; my heart trusts in him, and I am helped. My heart leaps for joy and I will give thanks to him in song.

PSALM 28:7

God's Exchange System

To all who mourn . . . he will give: Beauty for ashes;
Joy instead of mourning; Praise instead of heaviness.
Isaiah 61:3 TLB

Whenever we bow in real understanding before our Lord—whether it's at the cradle, the cross, or the empty tomb; whether we're seeing Him as Savior, Friend, or conquering King—we will long to give Him some wonderful, worthy gift. The Eastern wise men brought gold, frankincense, and myrrh!

But we know how it is, how it has always been. We come to Him dressed in the rags of sin—and He gives us His robe of righteousness. We offer our empty, broken hearts—and He fills them with healing love.

We bring Him needs—He supplies His endless resources. We give tears—He gives comfort. We give weakness—He gives grace. We cry out our fears and questions—He whispers His peace and purpose. We present ignorance wrapped in pride—He returns wisdom wrapped in humility.

He knows how it is, how it has always been, and yet He pleads with us to continue to come to Him and give all that we are and all that we are not.

Because He knows something else. He knows that when we have finally given Him all that we are and have received all that He is, we will at last hold the One Gift worth giving away.

Our gold is surrender; our frankincense, praise; our myrrh, loving obedience to His command to give as generously as He has given unto us. He receives such gifts with joy. (*WLT*)

Does the Lord delight in burnt offerings and sacrifices as much as in obeying the voice of the Lord? To obey is better than sacrifice, and to heed is better than the fat of rams.
1 SAMUEL 15:22

Through Jesus, therefore, let us continually offer to God a sacrifice of praise—the fruit of lips that confess his name. And do not forget to do good and to share with others, for with such sacrifices God is pleased.
HEBREWS 13:15–16

We know that we have come to know him if we obey his commands . . . If anyone obeys his word, God's love is truly made complete in him. This is how we know we are in him: Whoever claims to live in him must walk as Jesus did.

1 John 2:3, 5–6

Give, and it will be given to you. A good measure, pressed down, shaken together and running over, will be poured into your lap. For with the measure you use, it will be measured to you.

Jesus, Luke 6:38

I have no silver and gold, but I give you what I have.
Acts 3:6 RSV

Free from Misconceptions

Stand fast therefore in the liberty by which Christ has made us free, and do not be entangled again.

Galatians 5:1 NKJV

What daily doings—
    and undoings—
loosen the laces of
    our shiny Sunday shoes of
    certainty about God and His ways?
We learned to tie them—
    so proud—
    practicing carefully,
    seeking smiles.
But when life's riddles and pain begin to
    work loose those
    securely tugged knots that assured us
    of an easy, predictable life with God,

when we trip on our
    trailing laces
    and sit looking at their
    frayed and soiled ends;
when we can't keep things
    all tied up anymore,
dare we step out of our familiar
    shiny "pat answers" to
    walk on in Truth's barefoot freedom?
For our God is neither
    simple nor manageable,
but He is
    loving and trustworthy. (WLT)

Your righteousness reaches to the skies, O God, you who have done great things. Who, O God, is like you? Though you have made me see troubles, many and bitter, you will restore my life again; from the depths of the earth you will again bring me up. You will increase my honor and comfort me once again. I will praise you with the harp for your faithfulness, O my God; I will sing praise to you with the lyre, O Holy One of Israel. My lips will shout for joy when I sing praise to you—I, whom you have redeemed.
PSALM 71:19–23

Resurrecting Dreams

*The word of God is living and active. Sharper
than any double-edged sword, it penetrates even
to dividing soul and spirit, joints and marrow; it
judges the thoughts and attitudes of the heart.
Nothing in all creation is hidden from God's sight.
Everything is uncovered and laid bare before
the eyes of him to whom we must give account.*

Hebrews 4:12–13

The Lord has a way of looking into the very heart of things—especially the human heart. And there's no use trying to hide what's there.

One day I came to His Word with a nameless ache tucked away inside, troubling me, as it has been for several days. I read Luke's account of Jesus entering the town of Nain, where He came upon a heartbroken widow following the coffin of her only son.

> *When the Lord saw her, his heart went out to her and he said, "Don't cry." Then he went up and*

touched the coffin, and those carrying it stood still.
He said, "Young man, I say to you, get up!" The
dead man sat up and began to talk, and Jesus gave
him back to his mother. (Luke 7:13–15)

As I pondered what this story could possibly have to do with me, the Lord looked into my heart and said, "Something has died in you, Susan. What is this thing you're mourning and carrying in a coffin?"

I was startled, for I hadn't known that a funeral was going on inside me. But He reached out and touched the coffin that I was indeed laboring beneath, and I finally stood still and looked.

An important dream was being taken for burial—a dream the Lord knew I needed to have alive.

Very quietly, from within the depths of me, I heard Jesus whisper, "Do you suppose that if I can resurrect people, I can resurrect dreams too?"

I read the story again and saw the compassion, the power, and the *truth*. When our last hope is being taken for burial, Jesus sees, wipes away the tears of sorrow, and speaks *life* into our emptiness.

Praise God, He is the Lord of resurrection! The Lord of hope! In choosing Jesus as Savior and Lord, we have chosen abundant, eternal life. And it starts in *this* world. (WLT)

I have set before you life and death, blessings and curses. Now choose life, so that you and your children may live and that you may love the Lord your God, listen to his voice, and hold fast to him. For the Lord is your life.

DEUTERONOMY 30:19–20

I'm Growing!

Grow in the grace and knowledge of our
Lord and Savior Jesus Christ. To him
be glory both now and forever! Amen.

2 Peter 3:18

I keep reaching for You,
God,
and over and over I
find that
You reached first,
and so much
farther.
I keep reaching for You
Lord,
and over and over I
find that
I touch others
on my way to You.
I keep reaching for You,

Jesus,
and over and over I
find that
my arms are stretching.
I'm growing. (WLT)

I'm off and running, and I'm not turning back. So let's keep focused on that goal, those of us who want everything God has for us. If any of you have something else in mind, something less than total commitment, God will clear your blurred vision—you'll see it yet! Now that we're on the right track, let's stay on it. Stick with me, friends . . .

We're waiting the arrival of the Savior, the Master, Jesus Christ, who will transform our earthly bodies into glorious bodies like his own. He'll make us beautiful and whole with the same powerful skill by which he is putting everything as it should be, under and around him.

My dear, dear friends! I love you so much. I do want the very best for you. You make me feel such joy, fill me with such pride. Don't waver. Stay on track, steady in God.

Philippians 3:14–17, 20; 4:1 *The Message*

He Still Lights the Darkness

The people living in darkness have seen a great light; on those living in the land of the shadow of death a light has dawned.

MATTHEW 4:16

What was December twenty-fifth
before it was Christmas?
Just a chilly day
twenty-five sighs into an
endless winter night.
But when it became Christmas—
oh, when it became Christmas
it glowed!

A star, radiant and compelling, announced Christ's birth.
Yet it could not have been easy to find that baby beneath its
beam and realize that here was the resplendent miracle of the

ages—that this newborn's cry was the brilliant cry of salvation. For the Light of the World slid into our darkness with a whimper and a need to suck. Nothing regal here.

How astounding to enter that stable and realize that almighty God had dared to pour all of himself into dimpled arms and legs to be held in the arms of His creation. Perhaps God knew that if we could recognize and reach out for Him first in this dark unlikely barn, we would go on finding Him in life's dark unlikely days. He still comes to light our darkness. (NR)

It started when God said, "Light up the darkness!" and our lives filled up with light as we saw and understood God in the face of Christ, all bright and beautiful.

2 CORINTHIANS 4:6 *The Message*

Arise, shine, for your light has come, and the glory of the Lord rises upon you. See, darkness covers the earth and thick darkness is over the peoples, but the Lord rises upon you, and his glory appears over you. Nations will come to your light, and kings to the brightness of your dawn . . .

The sun will no more be your light by day, nor will the brightness of the moon shine on you, for the Lord will be your everlasting light, and your God will be your glory. Your sun will never set again, and your moon will wane no more; the Lord will be your everlasting light, and your days of sorrow will end.

ISAIAH 60:1–3, 19–20

I, the Lord, have called you in righteousness; I will take hold of your hand. I will keep you and will make you to be a covenant for the people and a light for the Gentiles, to open eyes that are blind, to free captives from prison and to release from the dungeon those who sit in darkness.

ISAIAH 42:6–7

This is how God showed his love among us: He sent his one and only Son into the world that we might live through him.

1 JOHN 4:9

Through him all things were made; without him nothing was made that has been made. In him was life, and that life was the light of men. The light shines in the darkness, but the darkness has not understood it.

JOHN 1:3–5

Who is it that overcomes the world? Only he who believes that Jesus is the Son of God . . . And this is the testimony: God has given us eternal life, and this life is in his Son. He who has the Son has life; he who does not have the Son of God does not have life.

1 JOHN 5:5, 11–12

Note to the Reader

The publisher invites you to share your response to the message of this book by writing Discovery House Publishers, P.O. Box 3566, Grand Rapids, MI 49501, U.S.A. For information about other Discovery House books, music, videos, or DVDs, contact us at the same address or call 1-800-653-8333. Find us on the Internet at http://www.dhp.org/ or send e-mail to books@dhp.org.